THE RENDERING
OF GOD IN THE
OLD TESTAMENT

OVERTURES TO BIBLICAL THEOLOGY
A series of studies in biblical theology designed
to explore fresh dimensions of research and to
suggest ways in which the biblical heritage may
address contemporary culture

Editors

WALTER BRUEGGEMANN, Dean of Academic
    Affairs and Professor of Old Testament at
    Eden Theological Seminary

JOHN R. DONAHUE, S.J., Professor of New Testa-
    ment at Jesuit School of Theology at Berke-
    ley in California

THE RENDERING
OF GOD IN THE
OLD TESTAMENT

DALE PATRICK

 FORTRESS PRESS Philadelphia

Biblical quotations, unless otherwise noted, are from the Revised Standard Version of the Bible copyrighted 1946, 1952, © 1971, 1973 by the Division of Christian Education of the National Council of the Churches of Christ in the U.S.A., and are used by permission.

COPYRIGHT © 1981 BY FORTRESS PRESS

Library of Congress Cataloging in Publication Data

Patrick, Dale.
  The rendering of God in the Old Testament.

  (Overtures to Biblical theology ; 10)
  Includes index.
  1. God—Biblical teaching.   2. Bible.   O.T.—
Theology.   I. Title.   II. Series.
BS1192.6.P38   231'.044   80-2389
ISBN 0-8006-1533-6   AACR2

8579B81   Printed in the United States of America   1–1533

To the Missouri School of Religion in honor of its eighty-six years of service to the Church and the University.

Contents

Series Foreword

Biblical theology has been a significant part of modern study of the Jewish and Christian Scriptures. Prior to the ascendancy of historical criticism of the Bible in the nineteenth century, biblical theology was subordinated to the dogmatic concerns of the churches, and the Bible too often provided a storehouse of rigid proof texts. When biblical theology was cut loose from its moorings to dogmatic theology to become an enterprise seeking its own methods and categories, attention was directed to what the Bible itself had to say. A dogmatic concern was replaced by an historical one so that biblical theology was understood as an investigation of what was believed by different communities in different situations. By the end of the nineteenth century biblical theology was virtually equated with the history of the religion of the authors who produced biblical documents or of the communities which used them.

While these earlier perspectives have become more refined and sophisticated, they still describe the parameters of what is done in the name of biblical theology—moving somewhere between the normative statements of dogmatic theology and the descriptive concerns of the history of religions. Th. Vriezen, in his *An Outline of Old Testament Theology* (Dutch, 1949; ET, 1958), sought to combine these concerns by devoting the first half of his book to historical considerations and the second half to theological themes. But even that effort did not break out of the stalemate of categories. In more recent times Old Testament theology has been dominated by two paradigmatic works. In his *Theology of the Old Testament* (German, 1933-39; ET, 1967) W. Eichrodt has provided a comprehensive statement around fixed categories which reflect classical dogmatic interests, although the centrality of covenant in his work reflects the Bible's own categories. By contrast, G. von Rad in his *Old Testament Theology* (German, 1960; ET, 1965) has presented a study of theological traditions with a primary concern for the historical dynamism of the traditions. In the case of New Testament theology, historical and theological concerns are rather roughly juxtaposed in the work of A. Richardson, *An Introduction to the Theology of the New Testament.* As in the case of the Old Testament there are two major options or presentations which dominate in New Testament studies. The history-of-religion school has left its mark on the magisterial work of R. Bultmann, who proceeds from an explanation of the expressions of faith of the earliest communities and their theologians to a statement of how their understanding of existence under faith speaks to us today. The works of O. Cullmann and W. G. Kümmel are clear New Testament statements of *Heilsgeschichte* under the aegis of the tension between promise and fulfillment—categories reminiscent of von Rad.

As recently as 1962 K. Stendahl again underscored the tension between historical description and normative meaning by assigning to the biblical theologian the task of describing what the Bible *meant,* not what it *means* or *how* it can have meaning. However, this objectivity of historical description is too often found to be a mirror of the observer's hidden preunderstanding, and the adequacy of historical description is contingent on one generation's discoveries and postulates. Also, the yearning and expectation of believers and would-be believers will not let biblical theology rest with the descriptive task alone. The growing strength of Evangelical Protestantism and the expanding phenomenon of charismatic Catholicism are but vocal reminders that people seek in the Bible a source of alternative value systems. By its own character and by the place it occupies in our culture the Bible will not rest easy as merely an historical artifact.

Thus it seems a fitting time to make "overtures" concerning biblical theology. It is not a time for massive tomes which claim too much. It appears not even to be a time for firm conclusions which are too comprehensive. It is a time for pursuit of fresh hints, for exploration of new intuitions which may reach beyond old conclusions, set categories, and conventional methods. The books in this series are concerned not only with what is seen and heard, with what the Bible said, but also with what the Bible says and the ways in which seeing and hearing are done.

In putting forth these *Overtures* much remains unsettled. The certainties of the older biblical theology *in service* of dogmatics, as well as of the more recent biblical theology movement *in lieu* of dogmatics, are no longer present. Nor is there on the scene anyone of the stature of a von Rad or a Bultmann to offer a synthesis which commands the theological engagement of a generation and summons the church to a new restatement of the biblical message. In a period characterized by an information explosion the relation of analytic study to attempts at synthesis is unsettled. Also unsettled is the question whether the scholarly canon of the university or the passion of the confessing community provides a language and idiom of discourse, and equally unsettled—and unsettling—is the question whether biblical theology is simply one more specialization in an already fragmented study of Scripture or whether it is finally the point of it all.

But much remains clear. Not simply must the community of biblical scholars address fresh issues and articulate new categories for the well-being of our common professional task; equally urgent is the fact that the dominant intellectual tradition of the West seems now to carry less conviction and to satisfy only weakly the new measures of knowing which are among us. We do not know exactly what role the Bible will play in new theological statements or religious postures, nor what questions the Bible can and will address, but *Overtures* will provide a locus where soundings may be taken.

We not only intend that *Overtures* should make contact with people professionally involved in biblical studies, but hope that the series will speak to all who care about the heritage of the biblical tradition. We hope that the volumes will represent the best in a literary and historical study of biblical traditions without canonizing historical archaism. We hope also that the studies will be relevant without losing the mystery of biblical religion's historical distance, and that the studies touch on significant themes, motifs, and symbols of the Bible without losing the rich diversity of the biblical tradition. It is a time for normative literature which is not heavy-handed, but which seriously challenges not only our conclusions but also the shape of our questions.

It is now clear that the primary questions in biblical theology concern method. One of the most important methodological issues is to find a language that is appropriate to the claims of the text. Our problem is to find a mode of articulation which avoids, on the one hand, supernaturalism that is frozen and violates the vitality of the text, and on the other hand, historicizing that is preoccupied with facticity and is therefore unable to make any meaningful interpretative claim which has continuing authority. It is to this difficult matter that Dr. Patrick addresses himself; and he finds his way between the temptations of supernaturalism and historicism with consummate skill. He will neither let the text be a fixed absolute nor will he relativize the text away from its faithful referent.

Patrick's book is, in fact, a fresh presentation of the God of the Old Testament. Although he is attentive to method and alert to its possibilities and dangers, the importance of the book is that it does not linger excessively with questions of method. It risks speaking openly of God and seeks to represent Israel's own open speaking about God. In order to do this the author takes his cue from philosophical analysis. He is concerned to find a "language game" that is appropriate to what must be said and to the one about whom it must be said. He proposes a quite different mode of discourse that respects both the character of the *text* and the need for a *contemporary assertion* of its claims. By attending to the form of language and the mode of discourse, Patrick extends form criticism to the forms and ways of language that are the forms and ways of Israel's speech about God. Specifically Patrick notes the artistic, dramatic quality of the text. He sees that this theological discourse is both an *artistic* formulation and a *dramatic* presentation. That is, the language of the Bible does not *describe* a being who exists outside of language, but evokes a being enacting his existence before us, engaging us in an I-Thou relationship, and stamping his identity upon our imagination. Thus Patrick brings to his work skills and sensitivities to see that the literature itself presents an alternative world, with a cast of characters who have their own authority and presence in a drama which is both literary and experiential in character.

Patrick effectively avoids the trap of projection. The God known here is not a creation of the literature, but is a presentation of a God already known. At the same time he avoids the danger of supernaturalism, which proceeds as if God were "out there," uninvolved in the dramatic portrayal before us. The God characterized in the text is not simply a creation of authors, but is one who has genuine reality apart from aesthetic imagination. Yet because this God lives in the imaginative world of the community, it is precisely the drama of the text which evokes God to a distinctive kind of presence.

That is, the work of literature is not to *create* God but rather to *evoke* God to a distinctive kind of presence. The author's primary term for this mode of theologizing is "render." God is rendered in a distinctive and identifiable role, so that God keeps the same part throughout the literature. The God so characterized fits none of the conventional systematic moves to which we are accustomed. Nor is this God a code word for "world processes." This God is rather the decisive agent in the alternative world of faith which begins in imagination and moves toward issues of value and power. But the movement is dialectical. It is also true that disclosure in issues of value and power liberates imagination for fresh characterization. This is God decisively free from and unrestrained by conventions either of history or theology. Thus Patrick writes in a mode peculiarly congenial to an affirmation of God's freedom, free to play God's own distinctive role in the drama of faith. This God is recognized ever anew in the events of history as the God already known, which events form a comprehensive action moving toward dramatic resolution. It is the text which permits this decisive linkage of "ever new" and "already known." Its dramatic power permits new surprises from an historical agent whose ways are already well understood by the community of faith.

In an unexpected way Patrick's argument leads him to the now central question of *canon*. That is, the literature is not a random collection of diffuse opinions and affirmations. It is rather a confessional dramatization that has coherence and consistency. And the substantive result is that the God rendered here has identity and consistency which may be discerned in his person, his acts and his speech. In a most refreshing way, Patrick utilizes his aesthetic sensitivities and his dramatic powers in the service of biblical theology. The result of his work is not an offer of fantasy, but a statement about the reality of God as confessed in Israel, albeit in a mode appropriate to the text itself.

What Patrick offers is bold and experimental. Its argument will not be adapted easily to Old Testament theology, in either the mode of Eichrodt or of von Rad. Indeed, his work is likely to be misunderstood by those who will insist on either of those standard ways. But his bold and imaginative work warrants the effort. It is a beginning that will require intense and sustained follow-up. And that is precisely the role of an Overture.

WALTER BRUEGGEMANN
JOHN R. DONAHUE, S.J.

Abbreviations

JAAR	*Journal of the American Academy of Religion*
BA	*Biblical Archaeologist*
BHT	Beiträge zur historischen Theologie
BZAW	Beihefte zur ZAW
CBQ	*Catholic Biblical Quarterly*
JBL	*Journal of Biblical Literature*
JR	*Journal of Religion*
SBT	Studies in Biblical Theology
TBü	Theologische Bücherei
TNR	*The New Republic*
VT	*Vetus Testamentum*
ZAW	*Zeitschrift für die alttestamentliche Wissenschaft*
ZTK	*Zeitschrift für Theologie und Kirche*

Preface

The thesis of this book is the product of some two decades of reflection and experimentation. Before we embark on the formal argument I believe it would be helpful and interesting to recount salient stages in its formation. We might call it the biography of an idea. Perhaps by recounting this story I can indicate more graphically than the formal argument allows what I am about and steer you away from some misunderstandings.

The story begins with my initial contact with Francis Fergusson's exposition of Aristotle's concept of action during my first year in seminary (1960). Certain specific statements in Fergusson's work, *The Idea of a Theater,* intrigued me with philosophical and theological possibilities. He discloses at the outset of the book that he believes action to be deeper than discursive thought. In his words, dramatic representation "at its best 'undercuts' both scientific and theological modes of understanding the life of the psyche."[1]

Following Aristotle, Fergusson maintains that drama represents *action.* After an exposition of a sample of Greek, Shakespearean and modern dramatic texts by means of this concept, he returns to define it in an appendix. He shuns an abstract definition in favor of a practical one:

> [The concept of action] is to be used to indicate the direction which an analysis of a play should take. It points to the object which the dramatist is trying to show us, and we must in some sense grasp that if we are to understand his complex art: plotting, characterization,

---

1. (Garden City, N.Y.: Anchor/Doubleday and Co., 1949), p. 22.

versification, thought, and their coherence. For this purpose practical rules may be devised, notably that of the Moscow Arts Theater. They say that the action of a character or a play must be indicated by an infinitive phrase, e.g., in the play *Oedipus,* "to find the culprit."[2]

Ever since reading this passage I have sought to distill from every play and story I come across its "infinitive phrase." I would ask: What is each character seeking to accomplish and how does it contribute to the course of events? How does each scene embody the action of the story and carry it forward? How does the outcome fulfill and frustrate the purposes of the characters? The answers to such questions became the key to interpretation.

In the same year I became an adherent of the biblical theology movement. G. E. Wright's little manifesto, *God Who Acts,* became the locus of much of my thinking.[3] I was particularly drawn to his general thesis that biblical theology "is a theology of recital or proclamation of the acts of God, together with the inferences drawn therefrom."[4] It seemed self-evident that biblical literature was a dramatic representation of events in Israel's history and that our theological reflection should correspond as closely as possible.

Wright inferred from his general thesis that the actual biblical narrative was to be construed as a report of or witness to a divine revelation that occurred in historical events. Revelation, that is, was located in events, not in the biblical text. Since the events were also the object of historical research, the science of history was an avenue to divine revelation. I accepted this view of the matter for more than a decade, and it was to prove to be a fatal ambiguity in my attempts to develop the concept of action.

Initially I believed that Wright's thesis needed only to be filled out to explain how God acts in history. In the context of modern historiography, the course of human history is attributed to finite causes and excludes divine causation. I wanted a philosophical concept that allowed us to speak of God's action working through finite causes. Fergusson's concept of action seemed to suit the specifications. A

---

2. Ibid., pp. 243–44.
3. SBT 8 (London: SCM Press, 1952). I might say that I was under the personal influence of two other leaders of this movement: James Muilenburg and Will Herberg.
4. Ibid., p. 11.

case could be made, I thought, for the proposition that historical process was dramatic in character and therefore that the literary critical concept of action was applicable to it. When the authors of Scripture depicted events involving God's acts, they were—I believed—representing the events of history as having an underlying movement, reducible to an infinitive phrase, with God as the subject. Their depictions could thereby be brought within the modern understanding of historical causation.

The concept of action also appeared to solve a number of other hermeneutical problems. By means of it, we could identify the element of continuity between the actual historical event, as reconstructed by critical history, and the Old Testament representation of the event. That is, I believed that we could presuppose that the action (expressible in an infinitive phrase) remained constant from historical events to biblical representation. This principle of continuity could overcome the problem that critical historiography was creating for a theology based on actual historical events.

Finally, the concept of action provided, I thought, a principle of unity for all Scripture. One important feature of the concept of action is its synthetic capacity. Each character acts in his or her own right, and at the same time participates in the action of others and in the overall movement of the narrative or drama. Likewise, each scene is real in its own right, but also is a phase of a larger sequence of events. It seemed to me that we could view the entire story of Israel with its God as making up one comprehensive drama with one action, with many scenes and acts. The many voices heard in the Old Testament could be treated as characters with their own action and yet as contributors to the comprehensive action of Israel's history.

I first attempted to outline this conceptual framework in a semester paper for a course devoted to the philosophy of history. I expounded the concept of action as a metaphysic of historical process. That is, I sought to show that life really does correspond to art—or at least to the underlying principles of artistic representation. Individual humans are, I proposed, to be understood as beings who achieve their identities by pursuing purposes in relation to others against the backdrop of natural process. The interactions of humans make up a process with a teleological movement. This teleological movement can be interpreted by faith as the action of God. The biblical story could be interpreted as a play within a play that reveals the content and purpose of the divine action running through all history.

I quickly discovered how difficult it was to translate this relatively simple scheme into a conceptually precise and comprehensive metaphysical system. My original paper was promising, according to the professor, but lacking in maturity. In the years that followed, I rewrote the essay every year or two in my spare time and pressured my wife and friends into reading it. Time and again I was disappointed by noncommittal responses. Finally, I submitted a version to a scholarly journal and had it rejected. After that I admitted to myself that I was not sufficiently equipped as a philosopher to develop a metaphysical account of historical process.

My real interest in the concept of action had never been metaphysical, but theological. I felt compelled to develop it metaphysically in order to employ it in the construction of biblical theology. This was itself ironic, and the irony was heightened by the fact that I was discouraged from applying it to topics in biblical theology until it could be expressed adequately in metaphysical terms.

I attempted to apply the concept of action to biblical theology only once during these two decades, in a paper for a course in Old Testament theology during my doctoral program. The paper was devoted to an exposition of Gerhard von Rad's Old Testament theology, in particular his concept of re-presentation of tradition.[5] Von Rad was in agreement with Wright that the "acts of God in history" are the true subject matter of biblical theology. Unlike Wright, however, von Rad concentrated his attention on the Israelite traditions that witness to God's acts. It is only as historical events are refracted through the minds which discern God's acts that they become theologically significant. In addition, the witness is not static, but constantly undergoes "re-presentation" or "re-actualization" to express the faith of later generations. Various stages of re-presentation are preserved in the final form of the tradition (our Old Testament text). In the paper I contended that the only continuity that von Rad would grant was the process of re-presenting itself.

As profound and enticing as von Rad's theology was, I desired

5. *Old Testament Theology*, 2 vols. (Edinburgh and London: Oliver & Boyd, 1962, 1965).

a much more substantial principle of continuity operative within Old Testament tradition and an objective referent for that tradition. I believed that we needed to speak of an action of God in actual history and a substantial continuity between the historical action and the confessional re-presentation of it. The task of the biblical theologian was, I believed, to penetrate to the action of God underlying the tradition and then to interpret each account as a dramatic rendering of this action.

Again I discovered that it was quite difficult to move from a simple scheme to a finished, well-supported system. Von Rad's theological principle seemed to grow organically from his scholarship, but my alternative was based upon a metaphysic of historical process. To avoid imposing a metaphysical solution on a hermeneutical problem, I believed that it was necessary to show that form critical and traditiohistorical methods and research could be enlisted in support of the concept of action. The result was cumbersome and convoluted. It seemed that I was butting my head against an invisible wall.

The decisive turning point in the story was an encounter with the thought of James Barr. Barr began undermining the biblical theology movement in the early 1960s, but I really did not appreciate the weight of his criticism until I and a colleague taught a course on biblical theology in the summer of 1972. We had chosen Barr's *Old and New in Interpretation* as one of our texts,[6] and as I proceeded to expound it for my students I found myself absorbing its theses. This was not easy, for I had been guilty of practically every conceptual flaw isolated in his book.

The critical thrust of Barr's book is that the slogan of the biblical theology movement, "revelation in history," is ambiguous and distorting. The word "history" in this slogan was, according to Barr, used equivocally. We meant actual events accessible to the historian when it served our purposes, but retreated to the narratives of the Old Testament when it seemed advantageous. In addition, our over-evaluation of history distorted our perception of the full range of biblical tradition and encouraged a surreptitious selectivity among texts. We were reducing the "many and various ways God spoke of old" (Heb. 1:1) to one way.

We were also confused and evasive in our assertion that God "re-

6. (New York: Harper & Row, 1966).

vealed" himself in historical events. Gerhard von Rad bracketed the question of whether God actually acted in history as we know it by restricting himself to Israel's confession. Wright affirmed that the revelation was in actual events, but when he went on to describe this action he seemed to retreat from divine interventions to a general providence. It was the interpretation of the authors and their community that transformed events into revelation. Thus, the two chief spokesmen of the biblical theology movement meant something quite different than the slogan "revelation in history" suggested.[7]

Barr's critique of the slogan "revelation in history" not only laid waste the conceptual framework with which I had been working, but it also intimated a way through the impasse that I had encountered. In particular, it freed me from the necessity of developing the concept of action into a metaphysic of historical process. If Barr was right that biblical literature cannot be classified unequivocally and comprehensively as history, logic suggested that it be approached as imaginative literature. Fergusson's concept of action was perfectly suited to the analysis of imaginative literature.

Throughout the period when I was seeking to define and develop the concept of action, I followed Fergusson in relegating the art of characterization to a function of the depiction of action. That is, I understood authors to design characters to fit the roles they were to play in the action. I recognized that Scripture rendered God as a character, but I was inclined to conceive of this characterization as derivative of the action attributed to him.

After absorbing Barr's thinking I happened across a proposition propounded by Karl Barth to the effect that biblical literature "renders an agent."[8] I immediately recognized the value of this proposition for my thought. It constituted a necessary complement to the concept of action. For there to be an action, there must be a character who acts. For biblical literature, in fact, the reality and identity of God is certainly as important as the teleological movement of the course of human events. Indeed, I finally came to the

---

7. See ibid., chapter 3, "The Concepts of History and Revelation."
8. *Church Dogmatics*, vol. 2, part 1 (Edinburgh: T. & T. Clark, 1936), pp. 271ff. See H. W. Frei, *The Identity of Jesus Christ* (Philadelphia: Fortress Press, 1967); D. H. Kelsey, *The Uses of Scripture in Recent Theology* (Philadelphia: Fortress Press, 1975), pp. 39–50.

conclusion that it was the identity of the biblical God which prompted the people of Israel to interpret the course of human events as manifesting his action.

For me the suggestion that biblical literature "renders an agent" (or subject) was a challenge to develop a theory of literary characterization applicable to the biblical depictions of God. My reading of literary criticism, however, did not yield a sufficiently general concept of characterization, so I was forced to devise my own. I was impressed with the fact that authors not only delineate the identity of their characters, but also evoke the presence of subjects with an inner life and conscious purpose. It was these two components—evocation of presence and delineation of identity—that came to constitute my theory of characterization.[9]

I took it to be a virtue of my approach to suspend the question of the reality of the God depicted in the Old Testament in order to work out the way the depiction itself was achieved. I wanted to be able to demonstrate that biblical God language does indeed evoke the presence of God and delineate his identity. If these claims could be substantiated, we could speak of the dramatis persona who exists within biblical literature without broaching metaphysical questions.

I did not intend, of course, to abandon claiming reality for the biblical God, but only to avoid developing a metaphysical conception of characterization and action. These should be left as literary concepts. But then the problem does arise concerning the relation of literature (or better, *this* literature) to reality. How can an imaginary being be accorded reality? My answer is that he convinces us of his reality. When we recognize who he is, we realize that he must exist in reality. When we enter imaginatively into his action, we realize that he must be active in our history as well. When we meet him as the Holy One of Israel, he has the power to evoke a religious response in us. Consequently, the imaginative process by which the presence and identity of the biblical God was established and maintained must be accorded the status of "vehicle" of God's self-identification in human history.

To reiterate, the concepts of action and characterization form the

9. H. Frei, ibid., pp. 1ff. passim, provided the two components, presence and identity, and I simply correlated them with literary phenomena.

backbone of this essay. It will be the task of the chapters that follow to demonstrate their applicability to the God-language of biblical literature and their capacity to evoke the presence and delineate the identity of the God whom we recognize as ours.

There are a host of people who have suffered with me as I groped clumsily toward the position set forth in these pages. At the head of the list must come my wife, Mary, who has had to read and evaluate every word written on the subject for the last twenty years, as well as listen to me prattle on about it. May she experience satisfaction as well as relief at the outcome.

My gratitude also goes to the members of the Columbia T-Society, our local theological discussion group. I read the germinal essay to them some years ago and an early version of several chapters more recently. Their receptive response and probing criticisms encouraged me to continue and forced me to sharpen my thinking.

The book is dedicated to the Missouri School of Religion, my vocational location for the last dozen years. My Dean Alfred Illing-worth and President Adrian McKay have been sure stays during these years, and my colleagues John White and Tom O'Neil have been constant conversation partners. Much of what appears in this book was tried out first on John and Tom over luncheon meals in the university cafeteria. It is sad that its publication coincides with the dissolution of the institution and probably the dispersion of the faculty.

If I were to mention all those who aided me at some time or other toward the position developed in this book, the list would be too long. Let me, then, restrict myself to people who have worked with me on the actual manuscript. Martin Buss read the germinal essay and has monitored my progress over the years. Recently, Richard Hocks of the University of Missouri-Columbia English department critiqued my employment of literary critical concepts.

Finally, I wish to thank the editor of the Overture series, Walter Brueggemann, for his yeoman service. I began pestering him with portions of the manuscript when it was still deeply flawed, but he saw promise in it and made concrete suggestions for revision. He continued to scrutinize the text minutely as the manuscript neared its present form.

If there is anything of value in the argument of this book, the people named deserve the credit along with me. The position is my own, however, and should not be imputed to them or to the thinkers named in the account of its formation.

DALE PATRICK

Introduction

In this essay I will attempt to develop a paradigm or conceptual model for biblical God-language. The paradigm that I am proposing is that of drama and the other mimetic arts. I am not simply saying that biblical literature can be *compared* to drama and the like, but that it *conforms* to the principles which govern the mimetic arts. If biblical literature can be differentiated systematically from other literary works, the differences do not separate it from the mimetic arts per se, but define its particular place within this broader category.[1]

The paradigm will be applied to that rather substantial and most consequential portion of Scripture that speaks of God. I have adopted the somewhat barbaric expression "God-language" from linguistic analysis. The expression has the advantage of being comprehensive and specific at the same time. In addition, it does not prematurely characterize the language, as would an expression like "language *about* God."

In the following section, I will introduce the chief concepts to be used in the study and pose the questions I will be endeavoring to answer. In the remaining sections of the chapter, I will identify the scholarly methods to be used or assumed in the argument, relate what we are doing to the discipline of biblical theology, and identify

---

1. I need to dispense with one objection from the start: Were the biblical authors conscious of the paradigm being proposed? For any number of reasons authors may not be fully conscious of what they are accomplishing or the rules under which they are operating. We can count them as implicitly conscious, however, if they do in fact exemplify the principles of artistic representation. In other words, the validity of the proposed paradigm does not depend upon establishing what was on the authors' minds, but rather how they actually performed.

1

the portions of the Old Testament to be treated in the course of the argument.

CHARACTERIZATION AND DRAMATIC ACTION

The two governing concepts of our paradigm are characterization and dramatic action.[2] By characterization I mean the representation of personages in such a way that they engage an audience's imagination, in essence causing us to entertain their existence as living individuals. By dramatic action is meant the representation of deeds and occurrences within a spaciotemporal framework, exhibited in such a way that the audience enters in as participant.

The thesis to be argued in this book is that the biblical God is rendered as a character and his acts are represented as part of a dramatic setting which enlists the reader's participation. It is rather common for expositors to compare the Bible to a drama and God to an actor,[3] but I know of no serious attempt to extend this idea beyond the level of an analogy to an actual paradigm. If one were to do so, one would have to show that biblical God-language conforms to the principles of characterization and that the actions he performs fit the description of dramatic representation. This is exactly what I propose to do.

When one proposes to show *that* biblical God-language conforms to the principles of characterization, one is invariably faced with the task of describing *how* it does. This means that one must identify the principles governing characterization and exhibit how God-language conforms. Part One of this book does precisely this. The overall argument aims at establishing *that* the biblical God is a character, but in the process we will discover *how* the characterization is accomplished.

Characterization will be broken down into two distinct components: evoking the presence and delineating the identity of a character. Chapter 1 is devoted to showing that the biblical God is rendered as present and describing how this is accomplished. Do the biblical authors speak of God in such a way that the reader enters into his

---

2. There are other aspects of the mimetic arts—rhetoric, thought, production, etc.—that might also be examined, but I hold these to be auxiliary to the two concepts named. Hence, they will not be isolated for independent treatment.

3. For example, Bernhard Anderson's little book for lay readers, *The Unfolding Drama of the Bible* (New York: Association Press, 1957).

thoughts and feelings? Are scenes presented in such a way that the reader meets a living persona in his speaking and doing? If the reader is forced to engage this personage, does this have any bearing on biblical theology?

Chapter 2 takes up the delineation of identity. Does biblical God-language impart a distinct impression of who the divine personage is? What sorts of traits define the identities of dramatis personae, and does biblical literature impute these traits to God? If it does, what does this mean for biblical theology?

In chapter 3, one aspect of identity delineation is taken up for special consideration. If we can show that God's presence is evoked and his identity is delineated, there is still the question of consistency of character. If Scripture were one work by one author, it would be relatively easy to deal with this aspect of successful characterization. Since it is the product of numerous authors over a millennium, it requires a careful and nuanced argument. What criteria would have to be met for the biblical rendering of God to be adjudged consistent? How can discrepancies and polemics be fitted into a claim of consistency? What sort of formative process of biblical literature would account for consistency of characterization? What significance would consistency of character have for biblical theology?

Part Two is devoted to the other leading concept of our paradigm, dramatic action. Again we confront the necessity of showing *how* the action of God is depicted in order to show *that* it fits the description of dramatic representation of action. We must, of course, decide what we mean by action and how it is represented dramatically. For simplicity's sake, we can say action is that element of a sentence designated as the verb. To represent a person's action, an author must render it as motivated, deliberate and purposeful and as having some effect on the actor and others. Since a character pursues a course of action in relation to other persons and a natural environment, an author must depict a person as interacting in a temporal (sequential) framework.

Chapter 4 inaugurates our study of the action of God by placing it within the interaction of dramatis personae. Does the biblical God enact his identity in the realm of pure essences or in the spatio-temporal world of human experience? With whom does he interact? What role does he play in these interactions? What does he contribute to the course of events in which he participates?

If the biblical God enacts his identity within the give-and-take of human affairs, specific events had to be depicted as due to his effort. Chapter 5 is devoted to describing the artistic means employed to evoke God's action and give it a decisive effect in the course of human events. On what cultural assumptions could the authors rely and how did they make use of these to establish the reality of God's intervention? Did they endeavor to show that an act of God was motivated, deliberate and purposeful? How can a contemporary reader appreciate the artistry of the biblical representation of action?

Chapter 6 takes up one specific mode of divine action: speaking. Should the speaking of God be distinguished from his acts? How is his speaking portrayed in biblical literature? If God's speaking is a mode of his action, can we define what sort of action speaking is?

The final chapter of Part Two addresses the problem of unity of action. Unity of action is parallel to consistency of character. The question is whether one can discern a unified action running through biblical literature, or whether God's action is episodic. Does the sequential, cumulative structure of the biblical narrative suggest a unitary story with a common action? Can the story be subsumed under a single definable action? Is there a denouement envisaged for such an action?

Part Three rounds off the essay by inquiring into the reality of the biblical God. If we have established our paradigm, we have identified the biblical God as an imaginary being. Is he only that, or can we confirm his reality? Does the biblical rendering of God require that we acknowledge his reality in order to entertain him as an imaginary being? Can his reality be confirmed by our experience of the world and of ourselves?

If the reality of the biblical God can be confirmed, how do we explain the reality of the one who comes to us by the imaginative process described in our study? Can a theory of inspiration be developed that accounts for this seeming paradox? What effect did canonization have on the rendering of God? How do Christians enter this drama?

From this brief description, you should be able to grasp the direction of this essay and the sorts of questions that will be occupying our attention. Before we embark, something needs to be said about the exegetical methods to be employed, the discipline under which the book should be subsumed, and the portions of Scripture to be treated.

EXEGETICAL METHOD

I need to say something now about the scholarly methods and theories that I assume and/or employ in the exposition of the biblical text. Little will be said about these in the body, so I want to brief the reader now.

The Bible communicates nothing without a tradition which preserves its texts, language, genres, framework of meaning and historical context. Any paradigm which claims that the Bible communicates of itself without background knowledge simply fails to appreciate the complex interaction of text and tradition. This interaction is patently obvious in the case of the text itself and of the language. It is just as true of what used to be called "higher criticism." The questions of authorship, dating, historical context, type of utterance and tradition behind the text always were important to interpreters of the Bible. Modern critical scholarship has simply provided more sophisticated methods and exhaustive answers to questions that precritical scholars also confronted.

A study like this must simply assume the work of text critics, philologists and lexicographers. For us, the same could be said of historians. The types of study that will play an active role in our analysis are source criticism, form criticism and, to a lesser degree, traditiohistorical criticism and canonical criticism.

The primary critical methodology informing this study is form criticism. By form criticism is meant the development of a scheme of linguistic types or categories under which individual textual units can be subsumed by means of identifying formal features. The end toward which the form critic strives is the identification of the linguistic action of each identifiable type of speech or writing, an outline of the range of possibilities within each type and a sketch of the changes or development each type underwent during the biblical period.[4] I

---

4. This definition is my own, but I would give credit to Claus Westermann for introducing me to the methodology and guiding me along through the years. There are handbooks describing the methodology, e.g., Edgar V. McKnight, *What Is Form Criticism?* (Philadelphia: Fortress Press, 1975).

will continually be drawing upon form critical evidence and hypothesis in the course of the study.[5]

The overall argument of the book could be classified as an extension of form criticism. We are *classifying* biblical God-language, showing that a significant portion belongs to a certain type of language, namely, characterization. Formal phenomena, like the address format of a passage, are enlisted as evidence supporting our classification. It might be said that I have taken seriously the cliche, "the medium is the message."

The results of source criticism are incorporated wherever they seem to have bearing on the exposition. The generally accepted theses like the Documentary Hypothesis and the division of the book of Isaiah into First, Second and Third Isaiah will be introduced without comment. The dating and locating of sources in their historical and cultural contexts, on the other hand, will not be significant to our study.

A valuable aspect of source criticism is its provision of *con*-text for a text. That is, attribution to a specific author/source associates a text with other texts sharing language, thought and narrative connection. This association allows the interpreter to subsume a large number of texts under a common theological description. In biblical theology, G. von Rad, H.W. Wolff and their associates have developed a method for determining the "kerygmatic intention" of an author.[6] My interests are not so much in the conscious "message" of an author for his time, however, but in the shared tradition and dramatic means employed. Once a writing was absorbed into the common tradition and combined with others, its particular point is blended with others, and the shared tradition and dramatic means become the enduring message.

You might say that I am attempting to balance source critical analysis and the sort of analysis advocated by Brevard Childs, who holds that exposition should be focused on the final form of the text.[7] He maintains that we should interpret the communication the

---

5. I will be ignoring the sociological aspects of speech forms.
6. See W. Brueggemann and H.W. Wolff, *The Vitality of Old Testament Traditions* (Atlanta: John Knox Press, 1975), for a statement and application of this method to the authors of the Pentateuch.
7. His massive *Introduction to the Old Testament as Scripture* (Philadelphia: Fortress Press, 1979) is an apology for this position.

text now intends, not the communication of its components. After recognizing the components, we are to trace the detemporalizing and blending effect of the tradition and to accord the result canonical status.

Our scholarship has facilitated encounters with living moments in time and with traditions in formation, and I am not willing to surrender these encounters. On the other hand, I do think we need to appreciate the detemporalizing and blending that has occurred in the formation of the canonical form of the tradition. To harmonize these two, I would accentuate that aspect of each source that contributes to the ongoing flow of the tradition and is still heard by the sensitive reader of the text.

I would certainly agree with Childs that the canonical form of Scripture is the locus for theological construction.[8] I understand this to entail the reading of the Old Testament as one work by many authors. As a single work, one would expect a certain consistency and unity. The theologian cannot force this unity and consistency, however, but must find it. It must be argued toward, not from.

Finally, I should mention traditiohistorical criticism. The concept of tradition plays an important role in the argument. It is used to explain the unity and consistency of the biblical rendering of Yahweh. On the other hand, I do not place great stock in the reconstructions of the oral tradition behind the text. The text is a written communication, and its design and nuance can be taken as intentional.[9] Consequently, I will speak of authors, composition and audience.

THE DISCIPLINE OF OLD TESTAMENT THEOLOGY

I have been referring to "biblical theology" rather frequently, so I had best explain what I mean by this discipline and how this essay fits it.

First, I should say that I consider the Old Testament to be an independent and integral Scripture, so it is legitimate to say that one is constructing a "biblical" theology when one limits the scope of study to the Old Testament. I will explain my position further in the last chapter.

8. See his *Biblical Theology in Crisis* (Philadelphia: Westminster Press, 1974), pp. 99ff. passim.
9. If various elements of a text are accounted for by means of the stages it passed through in oral tradition, one can lose faith in authorial intention.

Our current cultural setting allows great latitude in the use of the word "theology." One can discuss almost anything in almost any fashion under the rubric "theologizing." At a minimum, however, I should think that theology has something to do with speaking of God.[10] As an intellectual discipline, it should mean carefully supported, coherently ordered, and open-ended speaking.

When the adjective "biblical" is attached, one should mean a disciplined study of the God-language of the Bible or some segment of it.[11] By using this adjective, one is thrust into a tradition that circumscribes its content, sets its agenda, and passes on unsolved problems and unending debates.[12] If I were of a mind to define biblical theology thoroughly and precisely, it would be necessary to recount its history and describe the present state of the art.

I am not of such a mind; what I want to do is isolate one issue debated by biblical theologians and show how this essay addresses that issue. The issue I have in mind is the basic ordering of topics in a biblical theology and the reasoning behind it. The older theologies tended to follow a traditional doctrinal scheme, namely: God, man, salvation.[13] The procedure was to collect data from here and there that was relevant to the topic and construct a general picture of biblical thought upon the topic. One might add a developmental scheme to account for disparate evidence.

Walther Eichrodt and Gerhard von Rad inaugurated something of a revolution by challenging the cogency of the doctrinal scheme. Both sought a scheme more congenial to the structure and content of the biblical material. There is a dearth of general statements in Scripture

10. Speaking of God includes, it should be made clear, speaking of other matters that depend logically upon God-language, such as theological anthropology, ethics, etc.

11. In itself the title "biblical theology" does not decide the much debated question as to whether the task of the biblical theologian is descriptive or normative. This is best, for disputes within the discipline should not be settled by defining it tendentiously.

12. Gerhard Hasel, *Old Testament Theology: Basic Issues in the Current Debate,* rev. ed. (Grand Rapids, Mich.: Eerdmans, 1972), provides a helpful overview.

13. L. Köhler, *Old Testament Theology* (Philadelphia: Westminster Press, 1957) exemplifies this approach; E. Jacob, *Theology of the Old Testament* (New York and Evanston: Harper & Row, 1958) and Th. C. Vriezen, *An Outline of Old Testament Theology* (Newton, Mass.: C. T. Branford, 1958) vary it only slightly.

on the nature of God, man and salvation, and this fact should be taken into account.

Eichrodt did not depart entirely from the scheme, but reorganized it around a biblical concept, namely, covenant. Actually, "concept" is too weak a word, for he actually has in mind the theocratic constitution of Israel, a relationship. He orders his two volumes around three relations: God-Israel (covenant proper), God-world, and God-man (in general). Within these parts he tends to fall back into the doctrinal scheme.

Gerhard von Rad breaks with the doctrinal scheme entirely. His theology basically follows the order of the materials in the Old Testament itself.[14] He rehearses the story, providing what amounts to a running commentary on the witness to faith in the text. Israel, he maintains, thought in terms of historical traditions and it behooves the theologian to follow suit:

> It would be fatal to our understanding of Israel's witness if we were to arrange it from the outset on the basis of theological categories which, though current among ourselves, have absolutely nothing to do with those on whose basis Israel herself allowed her theological thinking to be ordered. Thus, retelling remains the most legitimate form of theological discourse on the Old Testament.[15]

The proposal of a paradigm for biblical God-language which I am making is not a direct contribution to the question of how a biblical theology should be ordered. It is, however, predicated on the search for a congenial order. The paradigm of mimetic literature seeks to grasp Israel's way of thinking from the inside. If we are successful, we will have contributed to the discipline of biblical theology.

A LECTIONARY

If one takes the canon of Scripture as the locus for biblical theology and pursues a topic to which a vast number of texts are directly relevant, it becomes apparent that a selection of texts must be made. It would be unfeasible to attempt to cover all or even a high percentage of relevant texts. Moreover, the argument will attain greater

---

14. Actually the LXX order: history, psalms and wisdom, prophecy.
15. *Old Testament Theology*, vol. 1 (Edinburgh and London: Oliver & Boyd, 1962), pp. 120–21.

simplicity and clarity if we concentrate on a few and return to them periodically.

Since the entire canon has been accepted as the locus for biblical theology, it seems appropriate to treat texts from each portion of the canon. I propose to limit myself to passages from Genesis and Exodus in the Torah; Isaiah, Jeremiah, Hosea, and Amos in the Nabiim; and Psalms and Job in the Kethubim. Since even this selection is too large, a number of specific passages will receive concentrated and recurring attention. Occasionally passages from other books will be cited when the thesis requires or is significantly enhanced by reference to a particular utterance. The introduction to each chapter will explain the logic of selection.

Although the discussion will be limited to portions of the biblical text, the reader will soon realize that I intend it to be comprehensive. The conceptual scheme presented is expected to account for biblical God-language as a whole, explaining all relevant utterances and their cumulative force. It is hoped that the texts to be expounded are sufficiently significant and/or representative to support such a comprehensive, ambitious thesis.

PART ONE

THE
CHARACTERIZATION
OF GOD

CHAPTER 1

The Characterization
of God

Few who are familiar with biblical literature would dispute the suggestion that Yahweh appears as a character in a significant portion of Scripture. He is one of the cast in countless narratives. Again and again he is depicted as thinking, feeling, deciding and acting. There can be little doubt that the writings of Scripture not only attach predicates to a subject, they "render an agent" (Karl Barth).[1] It is our task to make something of this literary fact.

To categorize biblical God-language as characterization, it is first necessary to define what is meant by "characterization." A literary character is simply a personage who plays a role in a dramatic sequence. Typically, playing a role involves acting and being acted upon, contributing to and reaping the consequences of the course of events in which he or she participates. To play a role, a character must have a reality in his or her own right. That is, a character must be depicted as a subject with presence and a concrete, consistent identity. It is this depiction of a subject that we call characterization.

Using the literary critical concept of characterization may suggest to the reader that the thesis of this study is really not so much biblical theology as biblical aesthetics. This impression would be mistaken. Obviously I hope to define and apply the concept of characterization sufficiently well that a literary critic would be satisfied. I want, however, to penetrate to a more fundamental level than that to which a literary critic aspires. The critic tends to focus on the

1. *Church Dogmatics,* vol. 2, part 1 (Edinburgh: T. & T. Clark, 1936), pp. 271ff.

specific communication of a passage and studies the devices employed by authors in order to determine the meaning more precisely. I hope to get behind the specific communication of passages to what an author must accomplish to communicate at all.

The literary critic may also want to cultivate the appreciation of a passage as an artifact of language. The biblical characterization of God, consequently, would naturally be subsumed under the art of biblical characterization as a whole or of a given author in particular. My interest is quite different. I want to appreciate the characterization of God as a mode of theological thinking and communication. For me, the characterization of God is not merely a device, it is the mode by which God enters the world and a people come to know him. The form of biblical God-language—i.e., characterization—is a constituent part of the message itself. Biblical literature elicits a personal relation between God and the reader. To read about this God, one must enter into his thoughts and experience the effect of his speaking and acting.

We might add, finally, that the "Bible-as-literature" approach has generally sought to be neutral respecting the truth claims of Scripture. I do not aspire to neutrality. I believe that the God rendered in Scripture has the capacity to convince us of his reality. To entertain this God as an imaginary character, one must finally recognize that he actually exists. Much of the specific analysis will be limited to the means by which he is rendered as an imaginary character, and could be accepted by nonbeliever as well as believer. However, the end toward which the analysis leads is the recognition of the reality of the one rendered.

Before we proceed to analyze biblical God-language, we need to hone our conceptual tools. The following section will reflect upon the art of characterization and prepare the way for categorizing biblical God-language as rendering God as character.

THE ART OF CHARACTERIZATION

For the sake of analysis, the art of characterization can be broken down into two components: evocation of presence and delineation of identity. By evocation of presence I mean the representation of a persona in such a way that the audience entertains his or her existence as a living being. To achieve presence, the author must allow the audience to enter into the thinking and feeling of the persona and to enact the persona's experience of himself and his world imaginatively. There are numerous devices for rendering the subjective life public. The thought process can be represented by directly recounting or indirectly suggesting internal dialogue. The actions of a persona can be represented from the standpoint of the subject. By such means, the observer's standpoint of the audience is overcome so that it encounters a living person. To use Martin Buber's language, the persona rendered by an author must become a "thou" inviting the "I" of the spectator into relation.[2]

By delineation of identity, I mean the representation of a character with definite personal traits, coherently related to each other and consistently manifested in speech and deeds. To experience a persona as "real" and to recognize him or her again, an audience requires a specific individual with a unique history, a set of beliefs and values, a disposition, manner, moral character with strengths and weaknesses, a physical identity and a social location. The composite of attributes belonging to the persona must, in addition, be synthesized into an identity that impresses itself on an audience as unique and interconnected.

The remainder of chapter 1 will be devoted to demonstrating that significant portions of Scripture evoke Yahweh's presence by literary means. The course of the argument entails the examination and exposition of representative texts to exhibit the thesis that scriptural God-language offers a dramatic characterization of the divine persona and to illustrate the process by which our proposal can be confirmed by exegesis of other portions of the Old Testament. Genesis 1—11 is an appropriate segment of biblical literature to use for demonstrative and illustrative purposes because it is here at the beginning that the style and tone of biblical God-language is set. Moreover, these chapters offer a uniquely vivid and intimate portrait of the one who accompanies us through the Bible.

To balance the detailed treatment of the Genesis chapters we will survey biblical literature in its broad outlines. The objective of this general survey is to show that the characterization of Yahweh con-

2. Classically articulated in *I and Thou* (New York: Charles Scribner's Sons, 1958).

tinues through large portions of Scripture and affects all Old Testament God-language.

Chapter 2 will take up the second component of characterization: the delineation of identity. In it we will show that the biblical depiction of God manifests certain personal and formal identity traits that enhance his convincingness and allow for continual recognition.

GENESIS 1—11

The task before us now is to examine the God-language of a representative portion of Scripture to determine whether Yahweh is rendered as a character. Genesis 1—11 is a suitable segment of biblical literature for this exercise. Here at the beginning of the entire biblical narrative the identity of the central character is established for all subsequent identification. At the same time, it is set off from the central story of the Old Testament—namely, the story of Yahweh and his people Israel—as something of a prologue. This independence allows the authors a certain freedom to represent Yahweh with a distinctive directness, vividness and intimacy.

The text is a composite work of several authors, chiefly the Yahwist (J) and Priestly Writer (P). The sources will be treated as standing in creative juxtaposition to each other, forming a composite, dialectic impression different from either account taken by itself.

THE ACCOUNTS OF CREATION

Gen. 1:1—2:4a belongs to the Priestly Writer while 2:4b–24 derives from the Yahwist. P presents a stately, austere account of the origin of the cosmos while J recounts the creation of humans and their world as an intimate, almost domestic drama. Each, I argue, employs the language of characterization in speaking of divine creation.

In the account, God is depicted as carrying on internal dialogue only once, when he prepares to create humans: "Let us make man in our image, after our likeness; and let them have dominion . . ." (1:26). Although P employs internal dialogue only this once, it is sufficient to establish the presence of the art of characterization. The reader is allowed a glimpse into the thinking of the actor behind the act. This glimpse is something of a dramatic high point in the chapter. It is a momentous occurrence for the Creator to make a creature in his own likeness, so we the readers are permitted to view ourselves from God's perspective.

Prior to the creation of humans, God is depicted as speaking and acting, but we are not allowed into his deliberation. The account forces an observer's point of view on the reader. The impression given is of a series of occurrences that are known to have taken place but that are beyond the capacity of the human mind to conceive.

The style of narration does communicate something about the Creator. The repetition of "let there be . . . and it was so" suggest a Creator who brings the world into being without exertion. The repetition of "and there was evening and morning" gives his action a metronomic quality. Here is a God whose power and intelligence surpass the capacities of the imagination, so all that we can do is "stand in awe of him, for he spoke, and it came to be" (Ps. 33:8–9).[3]

The account of the acts of creation does intimate the Creator's subjective life. In indirect discourse, we witness him taking delight in each creation ("and he saw that it was good"). We can imagine him admiring his work at the end of each day and at the end of the week. When he sets aside the seventh day as a day of holy rest for himself and his creatures, there is a clear sense of divine satisfaction.

To summarize, even the austere, formal Priestly account of creation depicts God's experience of himself sufficiently to evoke the presence of the subject behind the acts. These hints of intimacy are carefully balanced with distancing features to keep the God depicted from becoming too familiar.

The Yahwist's account of creation (Gen. 2:4b–24) is bold in its intimacy and anthropomorphism. The scene is the human world, not the vast universe. Yahweh's initial creative act is portrayed as an act of molding a figure from clay, like a potter molding a vessel. This is, of course, more than merely an anthropomorphic metaphor, for humans have a material makeup that returns to dust upon death

---

3. The description of the world before creation (1:2) juxtaposes a surplus of imagery to present a mood of formlessness and tension to be resolved by a decisive act of orderly creating. It does not detract from the depiction of God's power, but rather enhances it.

(Gen. 3:19). The uniqueness of Yahweh's creative power is manifested in his power to animate this clay figure. To depict this act, the author stretches the very anthropomorphic image of blowing into its nostrils (2:7) to the breaking point.

Each subsequent act of creation is depicted as Yahweh's providing for the needs of his creature. His creature needs something to do, and also a way to fill his need for food, so God creates a garden and grants the man the right to live at its expense. But what of the creature's social needs? Yahweh deliberates on this and devises a solution: he will create a helpmate. He mistakenly, however, creates animals to fill this role and subsequently admits his failure. It is as if Yahweh were proceeding experimentally, were discovering the nature of his creature as he goes along. Another delightful detail is Yahweh's curiosity at the man's name for each animal.

The full mystery of creation is evoked by Yahweh's creation of the woman. The man must be put to sleep and the woman created in secret out of material from the man's side. Here the author suggests the unfathomable quality of the creative act and the wonder of its result.[4]

The Yahwist's account might be said to start with the familiar—an intimate portrait of Yahweh employing vivid anthropomorphisms—and to stretch the images to evoke Yahweh's unique power and wisdom. Even so, divine transcendence is endangered by the author's willingness to describe the Creator with such familiarity. The tradition has balanced this rendering with the more remote deity of P. The dramatis persona that emerges in the juxtaposition is filled with dramatic tensions, but both renderings work to evoke the presence of one and the same Creator.

PRIMORDIAL HISTORY

In the narrative portions of Genesis 3—11, the Yahwist source predominates and the Priestly material does little more than supplement the flood story. Hence, there is no need to organize the discussion by source. First, we shall identify examples of depictions of

4. For a fuller exposition, see P. Trible, *God and the Rhetoric of Sexuality* (Philadelphia: Fortress Press, 1978), pp. 72–105.

Yahweh's subjective experience, then of his communications with humans, and finally of his deeds.

At least five citations of Yahweh's deliberation occur in the course of these chapters, two in the flood story and one each in the stories of the expulsion from the Garden, the illicit mating of divine beings and human women, and the tower of Babel. Let me quote them seriatim because they give such a strong collective impression about the mind of Yahweh.[5]

> Then the Lord God said, "Behold, the man has become like one of us, knowing good and evil; and now, lest he put forth his hand and take also of the tree of life, and eat, and live forever"—(3:22).

> Then the Lord said, "My spirit should not abide in man for ever, for he is flesh, but his days shall be a hundred and twenty years" (6:3).

> So the Lord said, "I will blot out man whom I have created from the face of the ground, man and beast and creeping things and birds of the air, for I am sorry that I have made them" (6:7).

> The Lord said in his heart, "I will never again curse the ground because of man, for the imagination of man's heart is evil from his youth; neither will I ever again destroy every living creature as I have done. While the earth remains, seedtime and harvest, cold and heat, summer and winter, day and night, shall not cease" (8:21–22).

> And the Lord said, "Behold, they are one people, and they have all one language; and this is only the beginning of what they will do; and nothing that they propose to do will now be impossible for them. Come, let us go down, and there confuse their language, that they may not understand one another's speech" (11:6–7).

These citations make up a strikingly homogenous group. The Yahwist relies upon this mode of representation to explain Yahweh's acts, principally his acts of judgment. In two cases (6:3; 8:21–22), the utterance itself puts the act into effect, while in the rest it precedes it to make the motive and purpose of the act intelligible.

---

5. The RSV renders Yahweh (YHWH) as "the Lord." For an explanation, see the study note on Exod. 3:14 in *The New Oxford Annotated Bible with the Apocrypha* (New York: Oxford University Press, 1965, 1977), p. 70.

What is important here is the dramatic technique itself. The author thrusts the reader into God's internal dialogue so that we can think and feel with him. The way he thinks, moreover, is itself highly dramatic. He expresses his fear that humans will usurp his power and prerogatives (3:22, 11:7). He experiences sorrow at the evil propensities of his creatures and remorse for having created them (6:5-7). When he promises to reverse the curse of the ground and to refrain from total judgment after the flood, there are suggestions both of sacrificial appeasement and resignation to the fact of evil—"for the imagination of man's heart is evil from his youth" (8:21). These bold depictions of Yahweh's internal dialogue are powerful, moving evocations of his presence.

The narrative also contains other, less direct suggestions of his inner life. For example, Noah is said to have found favor in his sight (6:8). At the height of the flood God remembered Noah (8:1). Such little details reinforce the impression of the character rendered in these chapters.

God's speeches to human beings have much the same force as the foregoing soliloquies, although their range is greater and the degree of revelation of God's subjective life varies. In the Priestly portions of the flood story, the subject matter of J's soliloquies is transposed into communications addressed to Noah (6:13; 9:1-17). Neither reveals God's emotional state, but they do explain his purposes and give instructions. Divine instructions are important, especially in P, for they have the symbolic force of giving evidence of providence and of establishing order.

Some divine communications, though clear in their wording, evoke a sense of mystery as to motive and purpose. For example, Yahweh's prohibition against eating of the tree of knowledge (2:17) is unmotivated and seemingly arbitrary. Since the reader knows that the power of discretion is an essential characteristic of human beings, the denial of this power is puzzling, almost sinister. The snake uses the absence of motive or discernable purpose to propose a sinister one, namely, God's envy and fear of humans (3:5). Yahweh's warning to Cain, following his arbitrary refusal to accept Cain's sacrifice, also evokes puzzlement by its illusive, provocative phrasing (4:6-7).

The conclusion of the stories of the first sin and the first murder are verbal actions of a special sort. They present investigations resulting in sentencing. In Genesis 3, Yahweh walks in the garden oblivious to the events that have transpired. When he realizes that something is wrong, he proceeds to flush out the guilty, to unravel the case by inquiry, and to pass sentence on each party. The scene develops so smoothly that the reader does not recognize that Yahweh has been thrust into a new role, that of judge. The depiction succeeds marvelously in evoking the capacity to ferret out the guilty and exercise his judicial authority over his creatures.

In the early chapters of Genesis, the Yahwist relies upon corporal images for depicting Yahweh's presence and absence, and for his capacity to effect changes in the physical world. Yahweh molds his creatures of clay (2:7, 19), walks in the garden in the cool of the day (3:8), clothes his creatures (3:21), inscribes a mark on Cain's forehead (4:15), and shuts the door of the ark (7:16). Such corporal action is vivid and artistic, if somewhat puzzling to the theologically minded.

At other points in the narrative, Yahweh is located in a different ontological sphere, namely, heaven (11:7), and his action is mediated through creatures and processes of the creation. Yahweh provides a child for Eve through the reproductive process (4:1), causes the flood by means of rain and/or releasing the waters below the earth and above the firmament (7:10–24), and shatters the unity of the human race by "confusing" human language (11:7–9).

A third strategy for depicting Yahweh's action has already been mentioned: he decrees a certain state of affairs and it comes into being simply by the force of his authority. The sentencing of the snake, woman and man (3:14–19), the banishment of Cain (4:11–12), and the limitation of the human lifespan to 120 years (6:3), are examples of this judicial mode of action.

It is worth noting that not only Yahweh's presence, but also his absence and inaction serve to render him dramatically. The conversation between the snake and the woman, the eating of the fruit, and the couple's reactions to their new knowledge all take place in Yahweh's absence. This absence is actually felt.

The examination of Genesis 1—11 has yielded the evidence necessary to affirm that the God-language of the narrative exhibits the art of characterization. The authors have evoked a persona by depicting him as carrying on an inner dialogue, as deliberating and reacting emotionally, as speaking to humans and acting upon them, and as effecting changes in the drama by corporal and indirect means. The reader becomes familiar with this persona and is prepared to meet him again in subsequent portions of Scripture.

SURVEY OF BIBLICAL LITERATURE

It would have been possible for the biblical narrative to exemplify the art of characterization in its God-language in the portion devoted to the primordial past—the age of the gods, so to speak—but to cease such characterization gradually as the story moved toward human history. In fact, however, the narrative continues to render Yahweh as a dramatis persona throughout subsequent segments. The vividness and intensity vary and the manner of representation changes, but throughout the biblical period the dramatic presence of Yahweh is sustained and his identity depicted dramatically.

Within the primary narrative strand of the Old Testament, Genesis through 2 Kings, the greatest intimacy and intensity are found in the Abraham cycle, the Mosaic tradition, and in Joshua and Judges, while the stories of Jacob and Joseph and the accounts of the monarchical era present Yahweh less intimately and intensely.

The divine soliloquy, which makes such an impression in the early chapters of Genesis, virtually disappears after chapter 12. In its place comes an ongoing dialogue between Yahweh and the patriarch and later, the mediator. The divine persona appears again and again to Abraham to issue promises and commands, and he intervenes to aid his chosen one and his family. The rather truncated Isaac cycle (Genesis 26) maintains this intimate intercourse of patriarch and Yahweh, but the Jacob (chapters 27—36) and Joseph (chapters 37—50) cycles are much more secular. Jacob's life is punctuated by a few dramatic encounters with Yahweh, but otherwise Yahweh remains hidden. The Joseph novella does not render Yahweh as a persona with presence at all, except as the course of history manifests a purposeful action.

In the narratives in which Moses plays a leading role, Yahweh's thoughts and promptings are continually before us and his actions are depicted vividly and vigorously. Yahweh's assertion in Num. 12:8, "With (Moses) I speak mouth to mouth, clearly, and not in dark speech; and he beholds the form of the Lord," is an apt characterization of the Mosaic tradition. Beginning with Yahweh's call of Moses, there is constant dialogue between them. We follow step-by-step Yahweh's strategy for procuring the release of his people from Egypt. His actions establish his glory in the eyes of Hebrew and Egyptian alike. During the wilderness sojourn, we experience the presence of Yahweh in every crisis, both as the one who takes care of his people and as one who boils up in anger. The event at Sinai renders Yahweh's presence in theophanic imagery and identifies the one who is present by means of covenant ritual, law, and tabernacle. Moses is allowed unique intercourse with God on the mountain.

Yahweh's dramatic presence continues to dominate the biblical narrative during the conquest and the period of the judges. During the conquest Yahweh guides Joshua and the people in strategy and brings about miraculous victories over insuperable odds. Behind his specific actions is the sense of his irresistible purpose to give his people a homeland. During the period of the judges, Yahweh's interventions become sporadic. Because, however, the narrative is devoted chiefly to his active moments, it maintains a lively and intense sense of his presence.

There is a significant shift in the God-language of the narrative beginning in 1 Samuel and continuing through 2 Kings. The dramatic depiction of Yahweh decreases and becomes more abstract. A peculiar turn of events may allow a sudden glimpse of his activity behind the scenes[6] and evidence of the inexorable working out of judgment may be couched in the language of divine passion (above all, 2 Kings 17). On the whole, however, Yahweh's inner life and dynamic involvement are no longer the subjects of the *narrator's* art; they have been bequeathed to the prophetic figures in the narrative.[7] That is, the dramatic rendering of Yahweh has largely passed from

6. Cf. G. von Rad, "The Beginnings of Historical Writing in Ancient Israel," in *The Problem of the Hexateuch and Other Essays* (Edinburgh and London: Oliver & Boyd, 1966), pp. 198–202.

7. Cf. G. von Rad, "The Deuteronomistic Theology of History," in *Studies in Deuteronomy* (London: SCM Press, 1953), pp. 74–91.

the narrative proper to the prophetic word, and beginning with Amos, to the prophetic books.[8]

Since we have been treating the art of characterization as a component of narration up until now, there is some question as to whether we can discern this same art in the nonnarrative literature of the prophetic books. The answer is an emphatic yes. The very form of the prophetic oracle renders Yahweh dramatically present, for the prophet speaks in the first person as Yahweh. When the prophet speaks, it is God who addresses the audience. We can term this mode of characterization "histrionic": the prophet *enacts* the part of God in the word he speaks.

When the classical prophets composed the word of Yahweh, they went beyond formally attributing the utterance to him; they also rendered his thoughts, emotions and intentions. Indeed, they did so with an intensity and intimacy equal to any portion of biblical literature. The audience is forced to enter into Yahweh's inner life and join him in his decision. The literature has, in fact, an uncanny power to make us—who are far removed from the original utterance—the addressees.

The prophetic rendering of Yahweh died out in the early postexilic literature. In its place we find anonymous protoapocalyptic passages in the prophetic books. In these, Yahweh's communication with his people at a specific moment in time is progressively replaced by descriptions of Yahweh's coming intervention, interspersed with prayers and words of warning and comfort spoken anonymously. Portrayals of the destruction of foreign nations and enemies abound, and obscure allusions to world-historical or mythological dramas replace the concrete details of contemporary history.[9] The outcome of these changes is the apocalyptic literature, which renders God as hidden and remote in history, dramatically, cataclysmically present in the unfolding drama of the end. It is as if the biblical God had no

---

8. The gradual disappearance of God as a character in biblical narrative reaches its conclusion in the postexilic books of Ruth and Esther. However, other postexilic narrative, in particular 1–2 Chronicles, preserves at least the semblance of the language of characterization, and Jonah actually offers a lively, fascinating characterization.

9. See P. Hanson, *The Dawn of Apocalyptic* (Philadelphia: Fortress Press, 1975).

more role to play after the exile than to bring the fulfillment of the divine promises given earlier.

Psalmic literature renders Yahweh as the one addressed or proclaimed. Lamentation provides the most intimate and vivid evocations of the biblical God. The supplicant accuses, questions and pleads with his God, and thereby projects an image of the one to whom he is appealing. The psalms of thanksgiving for deliverance retain much of the immediacy of the laments. Descriptive praises are somewhat more general and impersonal. They do present a deity who is able to enter into our stories as a dramatis persona, one with great force of character, grandeur, majesty, moral rectitude and solicitude toward those in need.[10] When the praise psalm breaks into address of God, the overwhelming presence of the object of praise shatters the respectful distance of worship.

The book of Job is narrative, the bulk structured as a drama. In the poetic drama, Job's companions speak in the language of wisdom, discoursing upon a remote and righteous deity who is dramatically remote as well. Job speaks in the idiom of lamentation, addressing God in accusing and protesting language, yet holding on to the hope of reconciliation.[11] God's presence is overwhelming in Job's mouth, hostile and inscrutable but paradoxically a source of hope and comfort. When Yahweh answers from the storm wind, we meet one of the peaks of Old Testament characterization. Here is a God who is infinitely distant, sublime, mysterious and awe-inspiring, yet attractive and tender.

SUMMATION AND THEOLOGICAL REFLECTION

In this chapter I have attempted to demonstrate that the biblical God Yahweh is rendered as a dramatis persona in biblical literature. The art of characterization was broken down into two components, evocation of presence and delineation of identity. In this chapter, I sought to show that biblical God-language evokes the presence of God. An examination of Genesis 1—11 found that God was depicted

---

10. For the identification and description of these psalm types, I am indebted to C. Westermann, *The Praise of God in the Psalms* (Richmond, Va.: John Knox Press, 1965), pp. 52–151.
11. See chapter 4 below.

as a persona who carries on an inner dialogue, who thinks and feels, and who projects a living presence through speaking and acting. A survey of biblical literature identified a large and significant portion of Scripture depicting God with intensity and intimacy. Our lines of evidence thus converge to confirm that biblical God-language renders Yahweh as a dramatis persona.

If we say that the biblical God is a dramatis persona of biblical literature, we have placed him logically in the same category as Hamlet, Lear and Ophelia—and the brothers Karamazov. Such personae are "imaginary beings." That is, an author gives them life by means of an artistic representation which evokes their presence and delineates their identities. They exist for the audience by being entertained in the imagination and cease to exist when the audience no longer imagines them to be present.

It would be false to leave the impression that the art of characterization is limited to fictional literature. The writing of biography and autobiography also relies upon this art. Boswell not only tells us the facts of Samuel Johnson's life but he also evokes Johnson's living presence with a unique identity. When William Butler Yeats recounts his own life, he has to imagine what he once thought and felt and depict this inner life in such a way that the reader can relive it imaginatively. The art of characterization is not in itself fictional, but comes into play wherever character is represented.

It should startle no one that Yahweh is rendered as a dramatis persona. The dramatic depiction of gods and goddesses is common in the religions of the world. The divinities of the ancient Near East were certainly rendered as dramatis personae. Myths, epics, prophecies, hymns and rituals present them as thinking, feeling, acting and being acted upon. When the authors of biblical literature took up the task of speaking of Yahweh, they simply adopted the form of god-language common to their cultural milieu.

This is not to say that the art of characterization remains untouched by the unique identity of Yahweh. There are, of course, vast differences between the type of story told of Yahweh and those told of the gods of polytheism, between Yahweh's intensity and intimacy and that of other gods, between Yahweh's incomparability and the similarity of the gods to one another and to finite creatures. Yahweh's identity and story transform the art of theological characterization in the very process of adopting a common way of speaking of deity.

If we recognize that biblical God-language employs the art of characterization, the anthropomorphic features of this language can be appreciated rather than disparaged. Recognizable qualities are necessary for the human mind to entertain any dramatis persona. For the depiction of Yahweh to succeed as art, he must exemplify the qualities of all dramatis personae. The use of anthropomorphic language does not result in the confusion of Yahweh and human dramatis personae, for Yahweh's unique, divine attributes also evoke his presence and delineate his identity. Yahweh is enough like other personae to be entertained imaginatively, sufficiently different to be distinguished fundamentally from all others.

The evocativeness of the biblical depiction of God is a key component of his capacity to convince us of his reality. When we read the story of his action, we are engaged by him. He encounters us as a "thou." When we realize that his capacity to convince us of his dramatic reality and to engage us in a personal relation must by his very identity insert him into every human story, we must accept him as our God or take offense.[12]

12. See chapter 8 below for the development of this argument.

CHAPTER 2

The Identity
of Yahweh

In chapter 1, the art of characterization was broken down into two components, the evocation of presence and the delineation of identity. The balance of the chapter was devoted to demonstrating that biblical God-language evoked the presence of Yahweh. In this chapter we need to consider the other component. I will endeavor to show, in particular, that the biblical God is rendered as a dramatis persona with a specific identity.

When we use the word "identity" in reference to persons, we mean those qualities or traits by virtue of which we can recognize particularity and sameness in time and space. From an observer's viewpoint, those qualities constitute the person's individuality, i.e., being a specific person distinguishable from all others. From the subject's point of view, these qualities belong indivisibly to self-reference.

DEFINING IDENTITY

The problem of defining identity has plagued metaphysicians and psychologists throughout the ages, but our task is more humble and manageable. An author must simply assume that the identities of persons endure and endeavor to depict characters with individual traits, coherently related to one another, and consistently manifested in dramatic situations. Our task is to become aware of the art of delineating identity and to examine biblical God-language to determine whether Yahweh is so delineated.

NEED FOR CONCRETENESS

There are several reasons why an author must provide his characters with concrete identities. First, a character must have a sufficiently concrete individuality to convince an audience of his or her reality. A character would be a mere abstraction if he or she did not possess the specificity of persons as we know them from experience.

Second, a character only becomes vivid and present for an audience as he or she exemplifies traits that excite the mind to identification. When an author depicts the thought process of a person, specific thoughts and feelings are portrayed. Only so can we enter mimetically into their act.

Third, the identity of a character must be manifested repeatedly and consistently to establish itself as defining the character essentially. Consistency facilitates recognition of the dramatis persona in each new appearance in the drama or narrative. If the audience were unable to recognize the character again and again, the story would lose coherence.

In addition, consistency of character seems to be demanded by the human mind simply to satisfy the mind's desire for coherence. Even relatively minor inconsistencies can distract us if we feel that someone has acted "out of character." A character who is represented with sufficient vividness and uniqueness to be grasped as a convincing, indivisible persona and with sufficient consistency to be recognized whenever he or she appears satisfies this love of coherence.

COMPONENTS OF IDENTITY

Let us briefly consider the components of a fully developed rendering of identity. A character has, first of all, what we might call "species identity." A human persona shares the physical, psychological, moral, intellectual and social traits of the human race. Just to identify a character as a human, for example, means that we attribute to him or her a body with a recognizable form. Physical identity alone differentiates a human from hobbits, elves and dwarfs, not to mention God, angels and demons. The same could be said for the other powers and limitations of this species qua species.

Species identity requires an author to delineate each member concretely. Since humans exist in bodily form, each human dramatis persona must be depicted as a specific body with an identifiable visage. A body also locates the personage in time and space and requires the author to adhere to the laws of temporal and spatial location applicable to humans. Each human personage also has specific intellectual powers, personality, moral character, and sociocultural context. An author must depict each person as having a specific disposition, manner, moral sensibility, set of beliefs and values, social class, and so forth.

Individuality can be described in terms of class characteristics, e.g., male, Jewish, Hebrew-speaking, small-town peasant, economically independent and politically potent, loquacious, easily angered but gracious, and so on. These class characteristics, however, must be given life by a depiction which enacts them dramatically. In addition, to be convincing, the class characteristics must be synthesized in a character whose concrete identity impresses itself on an audience as unique and indivisible.

The delineation of identity also requires that each persona have a history. Every act we do and every experience we undergo belong to our essential being. One is forever the person who did this and underwent that. An author must convince his audience that each of his dramatis personae has a specific biography and then he must weave that past into the selfhood of the persona.

Finally, a character generally has a name. If I am asked who I am, the first thing I will answer is my name. A name differentiates a person from others, intimates a history, and evokes the sense of an indivisible "I" which synthesizes class and species characters.

A LOOK AHEAD

In the balance of this chapter it will be argued that the identity of Yahweh was of concern to the authors of Scripture and that the components of a fully developed identity can be found in the renderings of Yahweh. The order of treatment will reverse the discussion of components in the preceding paragraphs. We will begin with the name of God, Yahweh, and its revelation to Moses. From there we will work back through the components: biography, personal traits, and finally species characteristics.

The textual focus of the chapter will be the call of Moses. When Yahweh introduces his name for the first time, he identifies himself as the God already known. The dialectic between "new" and "old" at this critical point demonstrates that the authors of Scripture were concerned with the identity of Yahweh and sought to maintain continuity of identity with the past. The same passages employ biography to identify Yahweh and establish a pattern for reviewing God's deeds to delineate his identity. Yahweh is also depicted in these passages as manifesting personal traits that impose themselves on the audience as characteristic of him. The persona manifesting this personality can be recognized again and again in the biblical narrative. Finally, in the call of Moses, Yahweh claims to be God and acts as a deity would act. His claim to exclusive deity transforms the species characteristics of ancient Near East deity into traits of his particular, concrete identity.

The thesis that the depiction of Yahweh as a dramatic persona requires us to seek consistency raises difficulties that demand a separate chapter. If biblical literature were the product of one author who was adhering to one speech form, the question of consistency would be relatively easy to resolve. Given the fact that it is the product of a tradition with numerous authors employing a large range of speech forms, the claim for consistency becomes much more problematic and requires the development of a number of concepts concerning the structure and dynamics of tradition. Chapter 3 will be devoted to this task.

THE REVELATION OF THE NAME

The introduction of the divine name "Yahweh" into the biblical narrative in the call of Moses confronts the problem of his identity as forthrightly as any passage in Scripture. Here we meet a "new" God who endeavors to establish his identity for the exodus generation. He does so by identifying with the deity already known to that generation and sketching a future in which they will continue to recognize him.

According to the Elohist and the Priestly Writer, God introduces his name "Yahweh" for the first time when he calls Moses to lead the people of Israel out of Egypt (Exod. 3:13–15 E; 6:2–6 P). P states openly that the divine name is new at this point: "I appeared to Abraham, to Isaac, and to Jacob, as God Almighty (El Shaddai), but by my name the Lord (Yahweh) I did not make myself known to them" (6:3). E does not say that the name was unknown previously, but he introduces it with a command-promise instituting its use: "This is my name for ever, and thus I am to be remembered throughout all generations" (3:15). Clearly E means to introduce the name for the first time here.

The introduction of a new divine name is no small matter.[1] A name belongs to a specific person. When the name is used, the person bearing it is evoked in the mind of those who hear or read it. When an author states "Yahweh said . . ." or "Yahweh did . . . ," he has identified the one of whom he is speaking. The listener or reader is predisposed to take him at his word. We will conclude only grudgingly, that we do not know who is being talked about when what is said does not fit at all the one who bears the name. The use of "Yahweh" throughout the generations of Israel, thus, was a significant force for maintaining his identity.

Although E and P are clear that a new name for God was introduced in Moses' inaugural theophany, neither sees this as the introduction of a new God, or of a new monotheistic religion, or of the true God for the first time. P unites the God of the patriarchs with Yahweh in the divine "I" (6:3). Likewise, E has Yahweh introduce himself precisely as the God of the patriarchs: "The Lord, the God of your fathers, the God of Abraham, the God of Isaac, and the God of Jacob, has sent me . . ." (3:15). Both authors are in essential agreement with J that one and the same God was known prior to and after the call of Moses.

From this observation we can enunciate a principle: Yahweh is always already known in the tradition. There is no real beginning to the knowledge of the biblical God. There is no moment when he enters human consciousness for the first time. He is depicted as the Creator, then as the God of primordial humanity, of the patriarchs and matriarchs of Israel, of Moses and the people who escaped from Egypt, and so forth. Each segment of the narrative works at establishing the identity of the God depicted in it with the God who is depicted in previous ones.[2]

1. It is worth recalling that Old Testament theologies customarily treat the name or names of God, e.g., L. Köhler, *Old Testament Theology* (Philadelphia: Westminster Press, 1957), pp. 36–58; E. Jacob, *Theology of the Old Testament* (New York and Evanston: Harper & Row, 1958), pp. 37–64; W. Eichrodt, *Theology of the Old Testament*, vol. 1 (London: SCM Press, 1961), pp. 178–305.
2. For example, the call of Abraham has a universal purpose appropriate to a universal God (Gen. 12:1–3), and this call is passed on to successive patriarchs (Gen. 26:3–4, 24; 28:13–15).

On the other hand, Yahweh's identification of himself as the "God of the fathers" is not sufficient for Moses. When he so identifies himself (3:6 E), Moses is dissatisfied and presses him for his real name (3:13). The God known in tradition does not appear to be enough to inspire conviction; he must have a particular name that belongs to him alone. Somehow the name, though there is as yet no association with it, adds to the identification.

The introduction of the divine name simultaneously institutes its use for ages to come. There is something of a promise given in the institution of the name, for it projects a future in which the God who speaks and acts in the present will continue to be recognizable. As long as Israel lives, it will know the same God and call him by the same name. The name thus reveals Yahweh as Israel's God even before he delivers them from Egyptian slavery.

Nevertheless, even when Yahweh divulges his own name, he makes sure to identify himself with the "God of your fathers, the God of Abraham, the God of Isaac, and the God of Jacob." He continues to build upon the loyalty and trust of the people toward the God already known to them. The people were being asked to risk their lives and welfare for his promise, so he had to provide grounds for certainty. His identity as a new God already known satisfies both the need to build upon the known and trusted and to arouse hopes surpassing the known.

Critical theory adds a further dimension to the call of Moses. It is highly probable that the term "God of the fathers" designates a plurality of deities.[3] This would explain why Moses insisted on knowing the deity's name. When Yahweh identifies with "them," they become "him." The act of identification introduces monotheism into the tradition and sets a pattern for maintaining it.[4] The recogniza-

---

3. The classical study: A. Alt, "The God of the Fathers," in *Essays on Old Testament History and Religion* (Oxford: Basil Blackwell, 1966), pp. 1–77. The bibliography of the discussion on this thesis is massive.

4. The propriety of using the word "monotheism" to designate Old Testament theology is a subject of much debate. I do so on the basis that the only deity recognized and depicted in Scripture is Yahweh. Cp. G. E. Wright, *The Old Testament against its Environment*, SBT 2 (London: SCM Press, 1950), p. 39: "The value of the word 'monotheism' lies in its emphasis upon *the most characteristic and unique feature of Israel: the exclusive exaltation of the one source of all power, authority, and creativity*." (Italics in the original.)

bility of Yahweh in religious traditions, including traditions of a polytheistic kind, was the hermeneutical key by which Israel selected, rejected, and modified myths, concepts and historical accounts passed down from ancestors or circulating in the cultural environment.

To summarize, the introduction of the divine name Yahweh into the biblical narrative in the call of Moses involves a dialectical process of identifying the new God by reference to the God already known and of qualifying the God(s) already known by the addition of a new identifying feature, the name Yahweh. This dialectic shows that biblical literature employs a component of characterization (naming) to delineate God's identity and to maintain it through time.

RECOLLECTION OF YAHWEH'S HISTORY

The depiction of Yahweh in the call of Moses also employs a biographical mode of identifying him and this mode of identification continues to play an important role in biblical God-language. By biographical mode of identification is meant the recital of Yahweh's deeds to render his identity and facilitate recognition. This type of language is a perfect illustration of the principle that God is always already known. When Yahweh is identified by reference to his past deeds, the reference evokes the memory of the God known in those traditions.

Biography is a necessary and significant constituent of personal identity. Every person has a history belonging to him or her alone. This history defines who the person is quite as much as does the person's body, personality, social position and group belonging. Indeed, one's past is an ingredient in these other factors of self-definition. Adequate characterization must give each persona a particular past. This past must accompany the persona like an alter ego through time.

Yahweh's past deeds function in much the same way in the rendering of Yahweh as a dramatis persona as does a human persona's biography. The God who confronts the reader in the narrative present brings his past with him. He is recognizable because he is the same as the one known in the stories of his deeds.

The call of Moses recalls Yahweh's past to identify him and

promises acts that will become central to his identity. We have already discussed the repeated self-identification of Yahweh as the "God of the fathers." Although this expression does not recall specific deeds, it does recall an historical past. Such recollection exemplifies a pattern of identification that accompanies the biblical God throughout the story.

The promise of deliverance lays the groundwork for the rehearsals of Yahweh's deeds isolated by Gerhard von Rad under the title "historical credo."[5] The Yahwist's version can serve as an example: "I have come down to deliver them out of the hand of the Egyptians, and to bring them up out of that land to a good and broad land, a land flowing with milk and honey, to the place of the Canaanites, the Hittites . . ." (3:8).[6] This promise is converted step by step into a rehearsal of Yahweh's past deeds as the story progresses toward fulfillment. The people begin the tradition of rehearsing right after the deliverance at the Red Sea (Exod. 15:1-18, 21) and it passes to the mouth of Jethro when he meets Moses in the wilderness (Exod. 18:1-12). In these joyful responses in immediate proximity to the event, there is more a sense of discovery of who Yahweh is than a recognition. Yahweh's deed redounds to his majesty ("he has raised (himself) high," Exod. 15:21, auth. trans.)[7] and proves that he is greater than all gods (18:11). His identity and status are still in the process of becoming fixed around the exodus.

The older Sinaitic accounts have Yahweh rehearse his deeds a number of times. The decalogue, for example, begins with a self-introduction, "I am Yahweh your God," and adds the self-predication, "who brought you out of the land of Egypt, the house of slavery" (Exod. 20:2, auth. trans.). The force of this self-introduction and self-predication establishes the identity of the speaker in

---

5. "The Problem of the Hexateuch," in *The Problem of the Hexateuch and Other Essays* (Edinburgh and London: Oliver & Boyd, 1966), pp. 1–78, particularly pp. 3–13, 41–48. The bibliography of the discussion of this thesis is massive.

6. Elohist: 3:9–12; Priestly Writer: 6:6–8. These two allude to the covenant making at Sinai, too. Exod. 3:16–17 probably belongs to the Yahwist, for it ignores Sinai.

7. The exact translation of *ky ga'oh ga'ah* is uncertain, but the context suggests *self*-exaltation.

preparation for his exercise of authority. Another passage has Yahweh recount his deeds to establish his stature in the eyes of the Israelites: "You have seen what I did to the Egyptians and how I bore you on eagles' wings and brought you to myself" (19:4). Yahweh calls the people to witness his deeds and decide to accept him as their God (vv. 5–6). In both 20:2 and 19:4, the identity of the God who enters into covenant is established as the one already known by his deeds.

As the story progresses, the past deeds of Yahweh grow to include the deeds of the wilderness period and finally to include the possession of Canaan. When Joshua calls the people together at Shechem (Joshua 24), the whole course of events from Abraham through exodus to conquest (Josh. 24:2–15, echoed by the people in vv. 16–18) can be called to mind to establish the identity of the God whom they are being challenged to own. The God whom Israel is called to serve is known in the telling of his story and their own story.

The rehearsal of Yahweh's deeds continues to identify him at each new stage of the story as the God who is already known[8] and is taken up by the classical prophets for the same purpose. When Amos, Hosea and their successors announced Yahweh's decision to judge his people, they found it necessary to show that the God who addressed Israel in this new word was the same as the God known in tradition. Amos 3:1–2 is a particularly pointed example of the use of history to identify the divine speaker:

> Hear this word that the Lord has spoken against you, O people of Israel, against the whole family which I brought out of the land of Egypt:
> "You only have I known
> of all the families of the earth;
> therefore I will punish you
> for all your iniquities."

The God who addresses Israel is the one who has known them and

---

8. The rehearsals are clustered at the edge of the land as Israel prepares to take possession: e.g., Deut. 7:17–26; 8:1ff; Josh. 1:2ff. However, we do meet them later, e.g., Judg. 6:8–10; 1 Sam. 8:8; 12:6–11; 2 Sam. 7:8–9, 10–11; 1 Kings 8:9, 16–21; cf. 1 Kings 12:28. These tend to belong to the deuteronomistic layer of the narrative, exhibiting its synthetic drive.

been known by them. History is reviewed to reinforce the existence of this unique relationship. The prophet establishes the identity of the God addressing them in the prophecy of judgment with the God already known in history and represents the present decisions to judge as the logical ("therefore") outcome of the relationship between them.

Yahweh's rehearsal of his past deeds is repeatedly juxtaposed in prophecy to the offensive, rebellious behavior of Israel.[9] Thereby it takes on a double function: It establishes the identity of the God who now speaks a word of judgment and forces the addressee to acknowledge the necessity of judgment because of the disparity between his righteousness and the people's response. We might say that the identity of Yahweh established in his deeds is the standard against which Israel's actions are measured.

To summarize, the call of Moses identifies Yahweh by reference to his past association with the patriarchs and to his forthcoming acts for Israel. As the biblical narrative progresses, the acts promised in the call become past deeds rehearsed to identify Yahweh and establish that he is the God who has been known in the past. This mode of identifying Yahweh follows him through the biblical narrative into the prophetic announcement of judgment.

PERSONAL TRAITS BELONGING TO YAHWEH

The depiction of Yahweh in the call of Moses projects a distinct personality that belongs to his identity. Yahweh's personal traits make him a vivid, living persona in the biblical narrative and facilitate continued recognition.

By personality I mean the enduring disposition and style of a dramatis persona. A character's disposition is a composite of predilections, prejudices, preferences, inclinations and tendencies in thought and action. A character's style consists of the habitual patterns of behavior and the rhythm of physical movement and verbal expression.

Without a style and disposition peculiar to him, Yahweh would

---

9. Cf. C. Westermann's discussion of the "contrast motif," *Basic Forms of Prophetic Speech* (Philadelphia: Westminster Press, 1967), pp. 182–85.

be an unconvincing abstraction, not a living character. The call of Moses provides sufficient examples of personal traits to bear out the claim that he is indeed a living character.

Near the end of the call of Moses, when Moses has tried a variety of evasions, Yahweh becomes exasperated: "Then the anger of the Lord was kindled against Moses . . ." (Exodus 4:14). Yahweh is here rendered as experiencing and manifesting an *emotional state*.[10] It is indeed rather common for biblical authors to evoke Yahweh's moods. In so doing, they give him vividness and concrete definition. Anger, in particular, is commonly attributed to him. The reader learns to expect certain situations to arouse his anger and recognizes him immediately when they do. This personality trait is so well established, in fact, that Yahweh's detractors (Marcionites old and new) simply epitomize his identity by designating him a "God of wrath."

Yahweh's first announcement of his plans to deliver Israel contains a motivation evoking his sympathy and moral character: "I have seen the affliction of my people who are in Egypt and have heard their cry because of their taskmasters; I know their sufferings" (3:7; see also 3:9; cf. 2:24–26). This is highly emotional language. Yahweh himself has felt what the people experience. Here is a God who is sensitive to human suffering and is impelled to do something about it. Here is a God who sees things from the victim's point of view. Such a personality is not described, but rather is projected in language evoking the experience of the persona.

These qualities of personality pervade biblical God-language. It is not accidental that the passage resonates with language belonging to crisis situations. The expression, "I have heard their cry," for example, recalls the lament tradition in which the human cry is answered by God's gracious deliverance, e.g., "Yahweh my God, I cried to you for help and you healed me" (auth. trans. from Hebrew, Ps. 30:3, RSV v. 2). This echo of other deliverances helps to convince us that Yahweh did indeed express this sentiment here. We are conditioned

10. I want to express my debt to Rabbi Abraham Heschel's defense of God's *pathos*, in *The Prophets*, vol. 2 (New York: Harper & Row, 1962), pp. 1–86. I cringe to think of how he would have reacted to my use of his plea, though.

by continued repetition to expect Yahweh's deep concern for the welfare of his creatures and compassion for those who suffer. The passage itself, once it becomes settled in the tradition, becomes a prime example of such concern and leads us to expect subsequent depictions of Yahweh in the same vein.

Yahweh's gracious disposition is a hallmark of his identity. Not only is he depicted as acting graciously, but graciousness becomes a predicate of his being. In Yahweh's theophany to Moses on Mt. Sinai, he describes himself as "a God merciful and gracious, slow to anger, and abounding in loving-kindness and faithfulness" (Exod. 34:6, auth. trans.). The biblical tradition has established a "center" of the divine personality which conditions and circumscribes all depictions.[11]

There is a *linguistic style* that identifies Yahweh. The reader learns quickly to detect language that belongs to the divine persona. Certain formal features define it and set it apart: Yahweh speaks in first person, using self-referential pronouns.[12] The perspective from which he speaks also belongs to his speeches alone. In the call of Moses, this perspective is evoked by the actions he proposes to do and the continual predictions regarding what will happen.

The divine rhetoric itself exemplifies Yahweh's majesty and resoluteness. When Yahweh speaks, it is a solemn occasion. The place where he speaks is itself "holy ground" (3:5). Although emotional, his speech is formal and austere. For example, many of the statements in Moses' call have liturgical language in the background. Moreover, Yahweh speaks to the point with an economy of words. The directness and simplicity evoke a sense of resoluteness and supreme authority. There is in addition a sense of urgency provided by the repeated command to go: "Come, I will send you" (3:10); "Say this to the people" (3:14, 15); "Go and gather . . . and say" (3:16); "You and the elders . . . shall go . . . and say to him (3:18);

---

11. Cf. P. Trible, *God and the Rhetoric of Sexuality* (Philadelphia: Fortress Press, 1978), pp. 1–5; also D. N. Freedman, "God Compassionate and Gracious," *Western Watch* 6 (1955):6–24.

12. He can refer to himself in third person or by name, a somewhat disconcerting element for a form critic, but perhaps not entirely out of keeping for a majestic personage.

"Now therefore go and I will be with your mouth" (4:12). Yahweh is literally impressing Moses into service.[13]

The list of features exemplifying Yahweh's disposition and style could be extended, but our discussion is sufficient to explain and substantiate the thesis that the depiction of Yahweh projects a concrete personality which leaves an indelible impression on the mind of the reader.

YAHWEH AS A DEITY

The components of identity that we have been examining up until now define Yahweh as a dramatis persona, but they do not distinguish him essentially from the other personae of the biblical narrative. Humans too have names, biographies, and personalities. Yahweh's name, history and personality are unique to him, but having these makes him like a human persona. To set him apart from other personae, we must turn to those traits that belong to him by virtue of his being a deity.

We are seldom conscious of the species traits of human personae because most of our literature restricts dramatic characterization to humans. When reading such literature, we simply assume the powers and limitations of our species and focus our attention on the traits that enliven and distinguish individual personae. Only when we read fables, fantasy, myth and science fiction do species traits carry the weight of identifying particular characters. Then we become aware of the traits that distinguish elves, dwarfs, hobbits and humans from one another.

The biblical narrative requires consciousness of species traits because Yahweh is set apart from and over against all other personae at this level. He is creator, others are creatures; he is without beginning or end, others are temporally circumscribed; he is not limited to the location at which he is said to be, other personae are body-bound; he possesses the knowledge and power to exercise sovereignty, others cannot control their destiny; whatever he commands is right

---

13. Rudolf Otto is so struck by this sense of urgency in biblical and non-biblical accounts of encounters with deity that he makes it one of the elements of the holy in *The Idea of the Holy* (New York: Oxford University Press, 1958), pp. 23–24.

and just, all others are beholden to his will. All interactions between Yahweh and other personae presuppose such antitheses.

These features that set Yahweh apart from all other biblical personae belong to him by virtue of his deity. They are traits attached to the realm of deity in Israel's Near Eastern milieu during the biblical period. They were species traits that could be attributed to practically any ancient Near East deity.[14] In polytheism, however, they could not be used to distinguish an individual. The revolution wrought by Yahwism entailed the assigning of divine attributes to Yahweh to an exclusive degree and thereby transformed them into traits of an individual dramatis persona.

DIVINE ATTRIBUTES IN THE CALL OF MOSES

In the following paragraphs, we will isolate and examine some divine attributes found in the call of Moses. The aim of this analysis will be to bring to consciousness the way such divine attributes facilitate the recognition of Yahweh and delineate his concrete identity.

The JE account of the call to Moses in Exodus 3-4 depicts one of the most memorable theophanies in Scripture. While herding sheep, Moses notices a miraculous fire and curiosity prompts him to investigate. As he approaches, a voice commands him to keep his distance and remove his shoes "for the place on which you are standing is holy ground" (3:5). Subsequently he hides his face to avoid seeing God.

The key divine attribute here is *holiness*. This is not a power, but rather a quality of Yahweh qua deity. It can be communicated to finite beings by association.[15] Here the area around the burning bush becomes holy because God is present (in a finite manifestation called an "angel" in v. 2). The presence of the holy God requires a gesture of respect and inspires fear of violating the divine mystery by looking.

One might say that the experience of the holy, inspiring such emotions as fear and respect, is a signal of the identity of the one present.

---

14. Cf. H. Ringgren, *Religions of the Ancient Near East* (Philadelphia: Westminster Press, 1973), p. 53.

15. Hence the root meaning of the Hebrew word *qadosh*: to set apart (from common use).

Whenever Yahweh enters the human sphere, he is so experienced. Within a polytheistic context, however, the encounter with the holy signaled only that one was in the presence of a divine being; it did not establish which one. When Moses presses God for his name, he is reacting as a polytheist. Only when Yahweh's exclusive claim to deity is well established can the experience of holiness be recognized as a trait of only one being. The interchange between Moses and Yahweh goes a long way itself toward establishing this identity.

Yahweh's claim to exclusive deity is made first in the call to Moses in Yahweh's identification with the "God of the fathers." When he identified himself as such initially, Moses could still wonder "which one?" Once the divine name was revealed (3:13–15), his insistence on his identification with the God of the patriarchs became a claim to be the one they worshiped in whatever deity they worshiped. It was such a claim that has issued in the narrative of Genesis which depicts only one deity throughout.

Yahweh proceeds to promise his people liberation from bondage and possession of a homeland, a promise which assumes that he has the capacity to deliver. It is assumed, that is, that he has *power* and *knowledge* superior to those who would oppose him. In the course of the dialogue, he substantiates his capability in a variety of ways. Most salient is his prediction of what is to come, e.g., that the Israelites will welcome the promise of deliverance but the pharaoh will resist (3:18–19). These predictions demonstrate Yahweh's capacity to foresee and to design effective measures against his opponents. He does not directly demonstrate his capacity to exert force against the pharaoh, but the signs with which he equips Moses (4:1–9) foreshadow the wonders he will perform before the Egyptian monarch.

The attributes of overwhelming might and perfect knowledge were ascribed to the deities of the ancient Near East. They are species traits that distinguish the gods from humans.[16] They are the sorts of attributes that inspired praise and supplication, and were celebrated in myth.

The biblical narrative, however, does not simply ascribe divine might and knowledge to Yahweh; it also makes the claim that he

---

16. H. Ringgren, *Religions of the Ancient Near East,* p. 53.

possesses them to an exclusive degree. Polytheistic historiography customarily depicts conflicts among the gods parallel to conflicts upon earth. Within the exodus narrative, there is no hint that there might be other deities which would counter Yahweh's action. As far as the narrative is concerned, the Egyptians are "godless." The only one opposing Yahweh is the pharaoh, and he derives his power to resist from Yahweh (4:21).

This brief analysis of divine attributes in the call of Moses is sufficient to explain what we meant by traits that belong to Yahweh by virtue of his deity. To Yahweh were ascribed the prerequisites of an ancient Near Eastern deity, but he laid claim to them in such a way that all other claimants were excluded from his class. As a result, the attributes that define him as a deity delineate him as an individual persona.

THE EVOCATIVENESS OF DIVINE ATTRIBUTES

The traits that belong to Yahweh as a deity work in tandem with his personality traits, biography and name to delineate his identity and evoke his presence. His holiness signals his presence and arouses a mimetic response in the reader. We are brought into an encounter with the Holy One ourselves in the depiction of his theophany. At the same time, we are conditioned to view every manifestation of holiness as a signal of the presence of only this one deity.

Yahweh's might and knowledge are the presupposition of his biography, personality and name. Only a deity could perform the deeds that make up Yahweh's biography. Only a deity could have a perpetual association with the people of Israel. Only a deity could define what is right and just by his response to situations. Only a deity who laid claim to exclusive possession of divine attributes could exercise the sovereignty that assures the fulfillment of his promises and makes his deeds in history decisive for the course of human events.

Although one might expect such formal attributes as power and knowledge to be too abstract and cerebral to evoke his presence, biblical depictions use them frequently in a most dramatic way. For example, in the call of Moses, Yahweh refers to his power in order to overcome Moses' fears: "Who has made man's mouth? Who makes him dumb or deaf or seeing or blind? Is it not I, the Lord?"

(Exod. 4:11). Yahweh claims to be the direct cause of every turn of human destiny. The rhetorical question transforms the idea into a direct encounter with the speaker. One might want to argue the idea, but the dramatic context makes argument inappropriate and even rebellious.

In this section, we have endeavored to anchor the divine attributes in the rendering of Yahweh as a whole. They work in tandem with the other components of characterization to evoke the presence and delineate the concrete identity of this dramatis persona.

SUMMATION AND THEOLOGICAL REFLECTION

At the beginning of the chapter, I identified a set of components in the delineation of character. The body of the chapter isolated and examined those components within the call of Moses. First, we examined the revelation of the divine name. When Yahweh divulges his name, he identifies himself as the God already known to the fathers and promises a future in which he will continue to be recognized. Second, we studied the references to Yahweh's past and future story. Yahweh has an identity which includes a specific biography by which he is recognized in the present and anticipated future. Third, we isolated personality traits that Yahweh manifests in the call of Moses. These traits evoke his presence as a living persona and stamp an impression on the mind of the reader for continued recognition. Finally, we examined the traits that belong to Yahweh by virtue of his deity. He appropriates the attributes of an ancient Near East deity and claims to possess these traits to an exclusive degree. Thereby, these attributes become traits of his personal identity and work in tandem with the other components of identity to delineate this specific, concrete dramatis persona.

The delineation of identity serves dramatic purposes. It aids in evoking a living persona and it facilitates continued recognition. The more complete and concrete a depiction is, the more resonance is heard when subsequent depictions conform to and recall it. Moreover, rich characterization is enjoyable in its own right. Cardboard characters make poor drama, but characters with depth, complexity and nuance make good drama. The mind takes delight in grasping the full identity of a character and being able to see how each trait coheres with the rest and how each act is appropriate to a character with this identity.

When the dramatis persona is the God of the community that reads the literature, the delineation of a full and concrete identity serves religious and theological purposes for the author and the audience. For the believer, getting to know Yahweh is getting to know one's world in its totality. This is the one to whom we have entrusted our lives and from whom we seek guidance and encouragement. For the majority of us who read the Bible, this religious purpose is undoubtedly primary.

But, you ask, how can we have faith in the biblical God once we recognize that he is a dramatis persona? Is he not reduced to a figment of the imagination? Is not the delineation of Yahweh's identity a requirement of the art form and of no value to the theological description of God?

My answer is that what is necessary to the mimetic arts should be taken as a clue to the theological interpretation of reality. If Yahweh must be given a complete, concrete identity to be a living, recognizable dramatis persona, then God must become a determinate reality in order to relate to human beings. If the biblical God can be rendered with internal coherence of character, dramatically appropriate to realistic dramatic situations and evocative of the sacred, he has the power to convince us that he is indeed the very identity of the one who confronts us as a determinate reality.

I will develop my argument in support of the reality of the biblical God in the final two chapters. It is now necessary to address the question of consistency in the rendering of Yahweh. Only if we can affirm that the rendering of Yahweh is dramatically consistent throughout Scripture can we say that biblical God-language is successful as characterization.

CHAPTER 3

Consistency of
Character

In chapter 2, the delineation of identity was described as the depiction of personae with a full range of concrete traits, coherently related to one another, and consistently manifested in dramatic situations. The focus of the chapter was on the traits that belong to Yahweh's identity. The element of consistency was set aside to be treated as a subject in its own right.

We can construct a working definition of consistency of character around two common English expressions: "in character" and "out of character." One is said to be in character when one acts consistently with previous behavior, and out of character when at odds with one's normal deportment. In the mimetic arts, it is considered an artistic defect for a persona to be out of character unless there is some dramatic reason for deviance (e.g., feigning madness). Defective characterization occurs, for example, when a character exhibits a talent he did not previously have and which did not develop in the course of the story.

For the rendering of Yahweh in Scripture to be artistically successful, the depictions of this dramatis persona would have to maintain the same biographical configuration, the same moral commitments and integrity, the same emotional disposition and style of comportment, and the same powers and qualities appropriate to one who claims exclusive deity. In a word, he would have to strike the reader again and again as the same God that the reader has come to know in the course of reading. On the other hand, if he continually jarred the reader's sensibility by behaving inappropriately, the literature would prove to be an artistic as well as a theological failure.

If Scripture were the creation of one author, the question of consistent characterization could be disposed of relatively easily. An author can be expected to maintain the consistency of every persona rendered. This affords continual recognition and satisfies the intellect's demand for consistency. If the reader found inconsistencies, they would simply be adjudged artistic defects.

The fact is, of course, that the Old Testament is a product of hundreds of authors, commentators and editors from a thousand-year time span. These contributors to the work lived in different places, drew on various cultural and theological traditions, and employed different types and genres for different uses. One would not even expect consistent characterization from such a diverse lot. Nevertheless, if we do not look for such consistency, we abandon the principle that all God-language in Scripture refers to the same deity.

The purpose of this chapter is to show that it is appropriate not only to ask whether Yahweh's identity is maintained, but also to determine if we can affirm that it has been. In the first section, I shall seek to describe what consistency of characterization is and how the depiction of Yahweh conforms to it. Then, in the second section, I will attempt to answer potential objections. A single identity emerges, I will argue, in a dialectical process that absorbs divergent, discrepant and polemical features into the portrait of the God already known. In the third section, I will propose a theory of tradition that explains the maintenance of consistency over a long, complex history of canonical formation. The chapter will conclude with a theological thesis based upon the argument of the chapter.

CONSISTENCY OF CHARACTERIZATION

We need to return for a moment to the contrast introduced above between "in character" and "out of character." When we witness a play, hear a story or read a novel, we intuitively adjudge a depiction as either in or out of character. In fact, we unconsciously accept a depiction as in character, but are made uneasy by inconsistencies. When we try to explain our dissatisfaction, we can usually come up with reasons. Others, however, may not agree with us and the argument may well turn on differing intuitions.

The reason it is so difficult to justify a judgment of inconsistency is that persons are not robots. They have the freedom to react differently to similar situations, to change their course of action, to fold under pressure, and so forth. A persona who is perfectly consistent is not very lifelike.

There are constants in human character, however, that set limits on fluidity. Each person's past is fixed and every new moment belongs to a person with exactly this past. Both nature and history bestow specific capacities and limitations on a person, and these restrict the range of possibilities for a person in any given situation. A person's disposition and style manifest themselves as surely as his or her facial countenance. As to moral character, consistency is considered a virtue and inconsistency a vice.

The art of characterization relies upon the constants of human character. Consistency of characterization—or consistent inconsistency—is used to build a strong impression of a persona. Strength of impression is an important factor in arousing interest and evoking the presence of personages. In addition, forceful characterization explains the action and interaction of the drama.

Consistency exercises such a force on characterization that depicting sharp changes of character is one of the most difficult feats of the art. To convince an audience that a character has undergone a conversion requires the demonstration that he or she was, in fact, consistent in the change.

CONSISTENCY IN THE CHARACTERIZATION OF YAHWEH

If there is a problem in defining what will count as consistency and inconsistency in the characterization of human personae, it is even greater for God. God is free from the constraints of finite existence. As one Scriptural passage states, "Yahweh is not a man, that he should change his mind" (1 Sam. 15:29, auth. trans.). Cynics charge, in fact, that with God "anything goes." When he acts according to principles of justice, he is honored as a just God; when he does not, he is honored as unfathomable in his judgments.

The problem of consistency already arises within the same work. The pentateuchal source known as the Yahwist (J) is generally credited with the authorship of both Gen. 3:8 and Exod. 33:19–20.

According to the first, Yahweh in bodily form moves among his creatures without harmful effect or even a great deal of spectacle. In the second, Moses is only allowed to look at his back ("for man shall not see me and live") and this is a special dispensation of grace. One must assume that the Yahwist, a consummate artist, sought and attained consistency of characterization. But if such radical differences can be said to be consistent, what will be counted as inconsistent?

Despite the problem in defining consistency as it applies to the characterization of God, it is quite unlikely that *any*thing was seen as compatible with his identity. This would have been intolerable to the communiy trying to be his people and to live according to his will. Again and again there are no's said to views of Yahweh. The prophetic movement, above all, says no to a host of conceptions and practices. Clearly, the identity of Yahweh was sufficiently distinct to provide an awareness of what was in and out of character. The task of the biblical interpreter is to recognize that identity.

The groundwork for recognizing the consistency of Yahweh's identity has been laid in chapter 2. We need only to review some of the components of identity discussed there and show that they were consistently maintained in the Old Testament. The revelation of the divine name exhibits the basic structure of biblical God-language. The entire Old Testament speaks of one and the same God. All utterances about deity refer to him. The actual name, Yahweh, is used constantly in all layers and types of literature. Even where the name does not occur, it is legitimate to say that such passages speak of Yahweh. It is one and the same God who is known wherever deity is encountered in Scripture.

The call of Moses provides Yahweh with a biographical identity. He is the "God of the fathers" and proleptically the God of the exodus, wilderness and conquest. References to this story recur throughout Scripture. Again and again the historians, prophets and psalmists identify who he is by what he has done in this particular story. To be sure, not all authors or works do so. It is possible that some prophets and sages did not personally think of him in those terms. It is doubtful, however, that any author conceived of God as incompatible with a biography. Even the most philosophical sage would have shared the community's faith that Yahweh interacted with his people in their story. Indeed, it is doubtful that any work which denied the exodus could have been accepted into orthodox tradition, for such a denial would be tantamount to repudiating Yahweh.

The call of Moses depicts Yahweh as manifesting emotions. He is motivated to intervene in Israel's behalf by an identification with their suffering and he is angered by Moses' resistance to his commission. That Yahweh did indeed experience emotions is assumed throughout the Old Testament. Perhaps there were sages in Israel who had qualms about such language, but even Proverbs and the wisdom psalms employ the language of approval and disapproval, and the Book of Job has one of the most emotional manifestations of Yahweh in the entire Bible. The particular emotions ascribed to him in Exodus 3—4—sympathy for the oppressed, anger with resistance or rebellion—are so characteristic of Yahweh that we expect them when the dramatic situation arises.

Finally, there are the traits that belong to Yahweh by virtue of his deity. That Yahweh possessed the power and intelligence to rule history and save his people was a matter of faith. Doubts do arise from time to time, particularly in the psalms of community lament (e.g., Psalms 44, 74, 80, 89), but the very act of speaking to Yahweh is an expression of hope that he has these attributes. If he were proved to lack them, he would not be the God he purported to be.

When Yahweh claimed to be the one true God, he claimed to possess all the attributes worthy of deity to a superlative degree and, by implication, to be without defect or limitation. This claim is openly and forthrightly expressed in the statements about Yahweh's incomparability.[1] The magnificent divine self-asseverations in Second Isaiah's prophecy epitomize these declarations, e.g.,

> For I am God, and there is no other;
> I am God, and there is none like me.
> (Isa. 46:9)

Other statements of Yahweh's incomparability draw out specific attri-

---

1. See C. J. Labuschagne, *The Incomparability of Yahweh in the Old Testament*, Pretoria Oriental Series V (Leiden: E. J. Brill, 1966).

butes. He possesses power and wisdom to a superlative degree (e.g., Exod. 15:11; Ps. 77:14; 1 Sam. 4:8; Job 36:22f.; Isa. 44:7). The greatness of his justice and righteousness and loyal care surpasses all others (e.g., Ps. 71:15–19; 35:10; Deut. 4:7; 1 Kings 8:23). His majesty and mystery make it impossible to fashion any likeness of the Creator (Isa. 40:18, 25; Jer. 10:16). Yahweh's incomparable divine perfection distinguishes him from all other personae—in Scripture or outside of it—and makes him worthy of being the only deity recognized in Scripture.

In summary, although it is difficult to stipulate the exact criteria for assessing the consistency of Yahweh's characterization, it is quite possible to show that the depiction of Yahweh in the call of Moses manifests an identity which is maintained throughout the Old Testament.

THE DIALECTICS OF IDENTITY

It is necessary, before we proceed, to confront evidence which might be construed as refuting the contention that Yahweh is rendered consistently in biblical literature. The position to be adopted is simply that neither inconsistencies, changes nor polemics in the characterization of Yahweh can be understood except by reference to a consistent identity. Without being able to identify the referent of a given depiction or attribution, it is impossible to say that it is out of character or in opposition to the norm.

It should be noted that in this discussion I have uniformly employed the term "consistency" rather than "continuity." If the reader takes these words as equivalent, my argument will be misunderstood. The opposite of consistency is inconsistency, or being out of character. This is an artistic defect, and I doubt there are many defenders of the inconsistency and inconstancy of humans and God. The opposite of continuity is "discontinuity." I believe that the biblical God acts to shatter the continuities of history, from oppression and violence to timidity and the empirical mind set. In some sense, this means that there are discontinuities in the rendering of God. The phenomena which we are about to consider fall mostly into this category.

The examples of divergent, discrepant and polemical depictions of Yahweh that I propose to consider do not fit into one pattern or come from one given portion of Scripture. They are simply challenges to my thesis that have come to mind or have been brought to my attention. Each presents its own problem and prompts an ad hoc solution. I shall begin with an example of a depiction of Yahweh that is indeed out of character. Then I will take up polemics against established traditions, tensions produced by the demands of narrative and tensions produced by changing sensibility. I will conclude with a reflection on freedom and consistency.

OUT OF CHARACTER DEPICTIONS

In close conjunction with Moses' call, we read the strange account of an attack on Moses by Yahweh (Exod. 4:24–26). Yahweh apparently assumes the guise of a demon who attacks at night for a violation of a taboo and is warded off by an apotropaic rite. This depiction does not fit well with the majestic, liberating God whom we have just met. It is little wonder that the precritical interpreters took recourse to rather radical expedients to harmonize the Yahweh of this passage with the Yahweh known in the tradition as a whole.[2] I think that it should stand for us as an inconsistency which makes us aware of how effective the biblical narrative has been in maintaining consistency. We usually accept the depiction so unconsciously that a passage like this performs a valuable function of bringing the entire process to our consciousness.

The biblical rendering of Yahweh could not tolerate many such jarring representations. The text is filled with surprises, and such surprises enhance the vividness and mystery of the biblical God. But surprises depend upon the capacity of the text to build up a firm identity that can absorb them. Let us take an example similar to Exod. 4:24–26. Yahweh's encounter with Jacob in a nocturnal wrestling match (Gen. 32:22–31) nearly shatters the identity of God, but Jacob's final confession draws the event back into the tradition: "For I have seen God face to face, and yet my life is preserved" (32:30). This statement, as it were, tells the reader to subsume the narrative under a category with which we are familiar, namely, theophany (cf. Exod. 24:11; 33:20; Isa. 6:5).

2. See Brevard Childs, *The Book of Exodus* (Philadelphia: Westminster Press, 1974), p. 96.

POLEMICS AGAINST TRADITIONS

In prophetic literature one finds rather frequent polemical challenges to known biblical traditions or popular extrapolations from those traditions. For example, Amos and Jeremiah challenged elements at the very heart of the tradition when they denied that sacrificial ordinances derive from Moses (Amos 5:25; Jer. 7:22). They were fully aware of the tradition and that added force to their denial. If Yahweh had not given the sacrificial law, there would be no point in his denying that he had.

This is a dialectical rendering of Yahweh's identity in the strictest sense. The prophets pose counterpoint to the tradition's point. The biblical God is the one who gave sacrificial law and who denies having given it. One cannot have the one without the other. God's identity is, in this case, genuinely paradoxical.

NARRATIVE REQUIREMENTS AND DIVINE INCOMPARABILITY

There is a potential for tension between attributes of perfection ascribed to Yahweh as the incomparable one and the dramatic characterization of Yahweh. Stories seem to require a significant degree of comparability among characters and this requirement seems to work against conformity with divine incomparability. H. Ringgren finds such a discrepancy between the language of ancient Near Eastern psalms and the actual depictions of the deities in myth that he doubts the intention of maintaining consistency.[3] If we were to concede that such a dualism exists in the biblical rendering of Yahweh, we would have to abandon the claim of consistency.

It is not necessary, however, to concede the existence of such a dualism in Scripture. Again one can observe a dialectic at work in the biblical text. There is one text in particular that sets out to explain how Yahweh's limited action exemplifies his incomparability:

> Thus says Yahweh, the God of the Hebrews: Let my people go, that they might serve me. For this time I will send all my plagues upon your heart, and upon the heart of your servants and your people, that they may know that *there is none like me* in all the earth. For by

3. *Religions of the Ancient Near East* (Philadelphia: Westminster Press, 1973), p. 53.

now I could have put forth my hand and struck you and your people
with pestilence, and you would have been cut off from the face of
the earth, but for this purpose have I let you live, to show you my
power, so that my name may be declared throughout all the earth
(Exod. 9:13–16, auth. trans.).[4]

To paraphrase, the upcoming plague will bring home to the pharaoh
and his people the full force of what they have experienced up till
now so they will realize that their opponent is the incomparable one.
Yahweh could have obliterated Egypt already, but he has held back
his power in order that there might be someone left to witness his
power and spread word of this incomparable one around the earth.

Stated in dramatic terms, a good story requires real resistance to
God's action, but his power is too great, if fully unleashed, to be
resisted. God must limit his power in order that the story of struggle
can be told. Perhaps the theme of Yahweh's hardening the pharaoh's
heart (9:12, 35, etc.) is meant not only to accentuate Yahweh's hidden control of the course of events, but also to make the pharaoh a
worthy opponent. If the pharaoh has received his power to resist
from Yahweh, it is a genuine power capable of generating a real
struggle.

This passage's solution to the tension between the requirements of
dramatic characterization and divine incomparability is not the only
one offered in Scripture, but it is sufficiently representative, articulate and subtle to bear the weight of the thesis that the two are
integrated and dialectically qualified in the biblical rendering of God.

Purging the Tradition

The requirement of language worthy of the incomparable God
exercised a purgatorial function on the language of tradition. Any
given moment in the history of tradition contained language and
conceptions that would strike later generations as unworthy. The procedure was not to eliminate all traces of the earlier language, but to
counterbalance it with newer formulations. The contradictory statements regarding Yahweh, asserting that he does and does not repent,
can be taken as an instance of such internal qualification. God's freedom to change his mind (i.e., to repent) and reverse his word was

---

4. The idea of using this passage for the present argument derives from
Labuschagne, *The Incomparability of Yahweh*, pp. 93f.

well established in the tradition (e.g., Gen. 18:22–33; Exod. 32:11–14; Deut. 9:7ff.; Jer. 18:1–11; Amos 7:1–6; Jonah 3–4), but at some time among some segments of the community change became a sign of imperfection. One passage is particularly fascinating. In 1 Sam. 15:29, Samuel asserts, "And also the Glory of Israel will not lie or repent; for he is not a man, that he should repent." Amazingly, the same chapter records Yahweh as saying: "I repent that I have made Saul king" (v. 11). The effect is quite paradoxical, presumably intentionally so.

Language adopted from Israel's religious milieu was also subject to internal qualification. For example, Yahweh seems to have appropriated the epithet and role of creator from the Canaanite El, perhaps El Elyon in particular.[5] In Gen. 14:18–22, Yahweh is explicitly identified with this Canaanite creator deity. However, the verb used in the passage for creation (*qnh*) occurs infrequently in Scripture. It seems to have had suspect associations, perhaps a sexual connotation, so the biblical tradition developed a new vocabulary (*brh*, *csh*) for Yahweh.

FREEDOM AND CONSISTENCY

At several points in the biblical text, Yahweh claims to be free of human limitations. The best known of these is recorded in Isa. 55:8–9:

> For my thoughts are not your thoughts,
>   neither are your ways my ways, says the Lord.
> For as the heavens are higher than the earth,
>   so are my ways higher than your ways
>   and my thoughts than your thoughts.

The declaration is made to justify Yahweh's offer of forgiveness (vv. 6–7), but it has often been generalized by exegetes and theologians eager to counterbalance literalism and dogmatism. I too find it a powerful theological insight. It should not be used, however, to deny the consistency or concreteness of Yahweh's identity. It should be remembered that it is an *utterance* of Yahweh, an act characteristic of him. Moreover, it gives a reason for his action, again a charac-

---

5. Cf. Labuschagne, *The Incomparability of Yahweh,* p. 109 and the literature cited there.

teristic of the dramatic rendering of Yahweh. It is in content an appropriate feature for the incomparable God. Here is a persona who possesses an identity like other (i.e., human) personae, but who transcends this identity to be who he is (and is who he is to transcend himself).

YAHWEH'S IDENTITY IN ISRAELITE TRADITION

The foregoing sections of this chapter have contended that the depictions of Yahweh in the Old Testament maintain a consistent, dynamic identity. Now I want to argue that the recognition of this God constituted the unifying force and external demarcation of the tradition which resulted in Scripture. As a consequence, the depictions of Yahweh throughout the biblical text should be read as working together to render one and the same persona.

The principle that I am developing here was articulated by James Barr: the tradition which resulted in the Scripture was "not everything that was said or passed on, but that which was passed on in a historical current in which it was recognized that the true God was known."[6] The primary evidence for this proposition is Scripture itself. In this work, only one God is recognized and all God-language refers to him. The authors who composed the works which were absorbed into the tradition, the people who passed them on, and the community that used the works and supported the institutions which embodied them shared, in varying degrees of intensity and orthodoxy, the conviction that only Yahweh should be honored as deity. If this were not so, we would have no work which exemplifies it.

Barr's principle is further confirmed by the terms used in Biblical literature for deities other than Yahweh. These deities are commonly designated "foreign gods" (*'thy ncr*),[7] "other gods" (*'lhym 'hrym*),[8]

---

6. *Old and New in Interpretation* (New York: Harper & Row, 1966), p. 89.
7. Gen. 35:2, 4; Josh. 24:20, 23; Deut. 31:16; Judg. 10.16; 1 Sam. 7:3; 2 Chron. 33:15; Jer. 5:19; singular: Deut. 32:12; Mal. 2:11; Hebrew Ps. 81:10, RSV v. 9.
8. Used 64 times in Hebrew Scripture according to Brown, Driver and Briggs, *A Hebrew and English Lexicon of the Old Testament* (London: Oxford University Press, 1907/1959); e.g., Exod. 20:3; 23:13; Deut. 6:14; 8:19 (+15 times); Josh. 23:16; 24:2; Judg. 2:12, 17, 19; Jer. 1:16 (+17 times); singular: Exod. 34:14.

or "strange god" (*'l zr*).[9] The deuteronomic preacher adds another, similar description: "gods which neither you nor your fathers have known."[10] The foreignness and unfamiliarity of these gods is due to their nonrecognition in legitimate Israelite tradition. As the biblical narrative and prophecy make abundantly clear, they were not really *that* unknown and foreign in fact. The point is that Israel, to the degree that it is true to itself, has no commerce or familiarity with any deity but Yahweh.

As one would expect, Yahweh is the familiar well-known God, the one who is "your God," the one who has been present and active throughout your history.[11] For the deuteronomic preacher, and by implication all biblical authors, the true Israel is the people of Yahweh. It is knitted together by the memory of this God's deeds. That memory provides him with the identity that makes him known, and it is *his* commandments and ordinances that Israel is obligated to obey by virtue of their association.

The contribution that this book makes to Barr's principle is our paradigm for the knowledge of Yahweh. The knowledge of Yahweh is the knowledge of his dramatic identity. The works of the tradition which communicate that knowledge do so by rendering a specific persona. These works made their way into the legitimate tradition because they successfully evoked Yahweh's presence and delineated an identity consistent with the rest of the tradition.

To visualize the process of tradition, we might begin with the position of an author who sought to contribute to the tradition. Like any author depicting any character, he had to render Yahweh with sufficient vividness to convince the audience of Yahweh's reality and to maintain a consistency of character through his own work. In addition, he had to make his depiction identifiable with the God already known in tradition. He drew upon the tradition which already provided God with an identity and had to represent "his" Yahweh in

---

9. Hebrew Psalms 44:21; 81:10; not used in the plural.

10. Deut. 8:3, 16; 11:28; 13:2, 7, 13; 28:33, 36, 64; 29:26; cf. 32:17. Other combinations, such as "gods of the nations" and "gods of the peoples" could also be cited.

11. Note the phrasing of Deut. 13:5 ". . . because he has taught rebellion against the Lord your God, who brought you out of the land of Egypt and redeemed you out of the house of bondage."

accordance with that identity in order to have his writing accepted into the tradition.

The tradition itself consisted of the written and oral narratives, songs, prophecies, sayings, etc., that were current and accepted at a given moment. Yahweh's identity was embodied in these materials and constituted the norm by which new pieces were judged and established ones reviewed. Every new contribution to the tradition itself became the norm for subsequent tradition and could even eclipse or modify earlier material.

A tradition requires a community that recognizes it as knowledge and an intellectual elite that studies, creates, disseminates and criticizes the items within it.[12] If the biblical God existed as a dramatis persona of the tradition, the community sharing the tradition would receive an impression of his identity and demand that all depictions represent him in character. The various elites would be the primary conduit of the impression and guardian of communal orthodoxy.

It is not our purpose to describe the process in all of its complexity. There was a wide diversity of groupings within the community and a diversity of elites and parties. The acceptance or rejection of candidates for tradition undoubtedly was deeply influenced by the conflicts and compromises within the community and its elite. To these factors would be added the experience of history, intellectual and cultural currents entering from outside and arising within, and so forth. The works that were accepted and are preserved in the Old Testament reflect these social and cultural factors. They have in common chiefly their capacity to render the God shared by all.

The entire people over the one thousand plus years of the biblical era shared in the act of imagining the identity of their God. No single author had the right to claim the character as his own creation. It was incumbent upon each author to draw his character according to the image in the common mind. This identity had the force of objective reality for the people living within the community of Yahweh.

If the tradition actually gave the identity of Yahweh the force of objective reality, it would be contrary to the nature of this tradition

---

12. On the social nature of religious knowledge, see Peter Berger, *The Sacred Canopy* (Garden City, N.Y.: Doubleday Anchor, 1967), pp. 3–51.

to isolate the individual works and treat each as if it were a world unto itself. If the writings of Scripture were included because they met the criterion of consistent characterization, it would seem that the most appropriate historical critical approach to them would be to interpret them as working in tandem to render the one God recognized in Scripture.

SUMMATION AND THEOLOGICAL REFLECTION

The art of characterization requires consistency of character. If the Old Testament employs this art to speak of God, to be successful he must be in character whenever he appears. It was argued in this chapter that such consistency can be discerned. It is to one and the same deity that all biblical God-language refers. He has a specific biography that is frequently recalled and generally assumed. He has personal traits that are regularly manifested and coherently integrated into the total identity. Finally, he possesses attributes appropriate to one claiming exclusive deity.

The identity of the biblical God, however, is not rigid or static. Rather, he is a persona whose identity emerges as dynamic, surprising and occasionally paradoxical, requiring of the reader a dialectical process of recognition. When a depiction borders on inconsistency, the interpreter must grasp it as a surprising manifestation of the one already known. When a depiction is polemical, the interpreter must recognize that the identity of Yahweh involves elements of paradox. When the divine persona claims to surpass all traits of human personae, the interpreter should realize that it is characteristic of this persona, and no other, to possess such freedom.

Since the scriptural rendering of Yahweh was the product of numerous authors over a long span of time, there must be some explanation of the maintenance of consistent character and justification for reading the depictions of different authors as working in tandem to render the biblical God. It was argued that the recognition of this God constituted the unifying principle and external demarcation of the tradition that resulted in Scripture.

The artistic requirement of consistency of characterization bears the weight of the theological principle of the unity of God. The supreme, ultimate reality cannot be at odds with itself or erratic in its manifestation. What is true, real, right and final must be the same for all eternity. Religiously speaking, faith requires that God's commandments and promises be knowable and trustworthy. If the believer cannot know what God requires and empowers, faithful living is an impossibility.

This artistic requirement also bears the weight of the unity of the canon. It would be possible to regard Scripture simply as an anthology of assorted inspiring works. The principle of canon, however, requires that the works be interpreted in relation to one another, as parts of one work. If the recognizability of God as the one already known was the essential criterion for inclusion in the canonical tradition, the unity of the canon has been established and the foundation of all relations between works laid.

The consistency of the biblical characterization of God, finally, provides a principle of unity for the history of Israel. The same God could be recognized in every new configuration and crisis in that history. The dramatic representation of each event and era was open to a depiction of God that was consistent with the tradition. In God we have the constant amid the changing fortunes of the people who recognized him.

Positing the consistency of the biblical God as the unity of the history in which biblical tradition took shape requires an inquiry into the action of God. Biblical literature renders God as a persona who interacts with humans and other creatures and achieves his identity in these interactions. To this aspect of the rendering of Yahweh we now turn.

PART TWO

THE ACTION
OF GOD

CHAPTER 4

Yahweh's Participation
in Action

One might imagine a deity who is so sublime that he or she is untouched by finite affairs, or who is so mysterious that nothing could be known of him or her. The God whom we meet in Scripture, however, is much more down to earth. He enacts his identity in interaction with human beings. We come to know him not by ascending to heaven in ecstasy or philosophic contemplation, but by looking with discernment into the tasks and conflicts of communal life. He is known in relation, not isolation; in interaction, not in eternal essence.

We must remind ourselves that this God who attains his identity in the midst of the human drama is an artistic achievement. The authors of Scripture employed artistic means to represent a human world in which God is an active participant. It is a sign of their success that the reader is able to enter this world imaginatively to such an extent that it seems utterly natural. Only when we step out of that world and begin to question the possibility of miracles and other divine interventions does the "constructedness" of the biblical world become apparent. If we can surmount our critical skepticism and arrive at a "post-critical naiveté,"[1] we can enter this world again, but in full awareness that it is an artistic and intellectual achievement.

In Part One, we treated narratives and other histrionic utterances as a function of the art of characterization. The story was, as

1. L. Dornish, "Introduction," in *Paul Ricoeur on Biblical Hermeneutics*, Semeia 4 (Missoula, Mont.: Society of Biblical Literature, 1975), p. 7.

it were, an occasion for the evocation of the divine presence and the delineation of his identity. These facets of characterization were isolated from the dramatic matrix in which Yahweh enacted his identity and effected his purpose.

Now in Part Two we shall shift our focus to the interaction between Yahweh and the other personae of the story. The subject remains the characterization of the biblical God, for his identity conditions and is conditioned by the interaction. Hence, we will still be examining the artistic means by which God is rendered as a dramatis persona. The shift of focus might be described as a turning from the persona himself to his role in the drama. We will be examining his interaction with others and the artistic means employed to convince the reader that he is an active agent.

THE CONCEPT OF ACTION

The word "action" is so important to the discussion of Yahweh's dramatic role that I need to explain at the outset what I mean by it.[2] I mean by "action" nothing more mysterious than what we designate by verbs. When Fergusson says that the action of a character or a play can be denoted by an infinitive phrase,[3] he is simply suggesting a practical technique for focusing the mind on the phenomenon portrayed. This technique involves nothing more than finding a verb that describes what the characters, singly and collectively, do.

Practically anything that can be designated by a verb can be represented dramatically.[4] The task of the author is to dramatize the verb in such a way that the audience enacts it imaginatively. If a character leaps onto a moving train, the author (or actor) must involve us in the struggle. If a character plots the humiliation of an obnoxious rival, we must be made to feel the motives involved and relish the projected satisfaction.

An author cannot, of course, render every act of his or her story with equal vividness and intimacy. A selection must be made and

2. The reader should recall the importance the concept of action had in the formation of the argument of this book as explained in the preface.

3. *The Idea of a Theater* (Garden City, N.Y.: Anchor/Doubleday & Co., 1949), p. 244.

4. For practical reasons, I will restrict the discussion to the action of self-conscious subjects.

a distance established. Some actions will only be reported. Some will be rendered in part and the audience left to fill in the rest. The force of a story's dramatization will depend on the evocation of the "feel" of selected actions and the convincingness of the background.

The author must correlate action with characterization. Actions must be appropriate to the characters to whom they are ascribed. The audience will be puzzled or unconvinced by an action that is out of character. Conversely, every action convincingly ascribed to a persona enters his or her identity and subsequent behavior must be consistent with it.

The author must also show respect for the logic of sequence. Aristotle speaks of a course of action as having a necessity about it.[5] Planning precedes execution, and execution must follow certain steps. In our example, the man who plots the humiliation of an obnoxious rival must design a scene, perhaps enlist others, draw the victim in, etc. Successful art convinces us of the inevitability of the sequence. If something goes awry, we must be convinced that the deviation from expectation is possible.

Before we proceed to examine the rendering of Yahweh's action, we need to distinguish between two different but related referents to the word "action." In English, we employ the word both for the purposeful behavior of a person and for the interaction of persons. Sentences ascribing actions to individuals are one of the most common types in our language. When we ascribe an action to an individual, we generally mean motivated, deliberate, purposeful behavior that effects some change in the situation of the actor and of those who are related to him or her. Expressions like "pursue purposes" and "seek satisfaction" are suitable substitutes for this meaning of action.

We can also speak of "participating in the action," or more colloquially, "getting into the act." Here the term denotes the web of interaction made up of the purposes and cross-purposes of many individuals. We have other expressions, like "get into the arena" and "join the fray," that approximate this second meaning.

In this and the following chapters, I have found it convenient to

5. *The Rhetoric and The Poetics* (New York: Modern Library, 1954), pp. 234–35.

treat the interaction of Yahweh with others separately from the action of Yahweh. In this chapter, we will be considering the aspect of interaction; hence it is entitled "participation in action." I hope to show that Yahweh is rendered as one member of the cast among others, so that when we examine the depiction of his interventions (in chapters 5 and 6), we will not lose sight of the interactive quality of his deeds and words.

THE WHO, WHEN, AND WHERE OF ACTION

The rather clumsy title does not mean quite what it might suggest. We are not interested in identifying any particular person, time and place. These obviously vary from story to story. Rather, the interest is in the *type* of persona, time and place that one finds in biblical narrative. The examination of type will lead to a fundamental distinction between biblical narrative and the myth and epic of Israel's cultural milieu.

The myths of the ancient Near East and of all polytheistic religions depict the interaction of a multiplicity of deities. The events depicted take place in a transcendent realm and in a type of time with laws different from the irreversible, ever-changing temporality of human experience. The epics of the same cultural milieu do include human personae, but these are of superhuman proportions. The time and space of epic are human, but the scene can shift to heaven, the underworld or enchanted places, and characters enter the altered temporality of these other realms. In the biblical narrative, Yahweh interacts only with human personae. The events of these narratives occur at places humans continue to frequent and within the same temporal sequence as the present.

The distinctiveness of the biblical story in these respects derives from the identity of Yahweh. When Yahweh claims to possess the attributes of deity to an exclusive degree, he effectively banishes from his story all other claimants to deity.[6] Only humans are left to interact with him.[7]

---

6. There are, of course, vestiges of polytheism, e.g., Gen. 6:1–4; Psalm 82; and Job 1—2, but such vestiges are marginal and lend themselves to an monotheistic account of reality.

7. There is one example of a nonhuman persona, the snake in Genesis 3, but the general absence of such figures is impressive.

Not only does the biblical narrative restrict interaction to Yahweh and his human creatures, the scene and characterization are remarkably historylike.[8] In Genesis 1—11, we have stories which once had the features of myth, but they have been largely demythologized. The Garden of Eden and the primal man still have mythical qualities, but one is struck with how moderate and realistic the account is when it is compared to parallel materials in Ezekiel 28. Again, there is nothing so otherwordly in the Noah story as the reward of immortal life given to Utnapishtim in the Gilgamesh epic.[9]

Beginning with Genesis 12, the narrative moves firmly within the horizons of historical life. There is a debate as to how historical the personae and actions of Genesis 12—50 are, but there can be little question of the historylikeness of the depiction. The individuals live among others, exhibit everyday concerns and needs, respond naturally to occurrences, and so forth. In addition, specific locations, political conditions, economic patterns, and legal customs locate the action in a particular period of history.

To account for the historical realism of the biblical narrative, I would again take recourse to the identity of the biblical God.[10] One might say that there is a respect shown the conditions of creaturely existence. There is no depreciation of spaciotemporal life over against the ideal world of deity. Yahweh does belong to a transcendent realm, but the narrative is silent about existence there.[11] As God's good creation, the world inhabited by humans is worthy of careful, unsentimental depiction.

One might add that the biblical depiction of the human scene is not, with a few exceptions, idealized. Yahweh is not allowed to

---

8. A term borrowed from H. Frei, *The Eclipse of Biblical Narrative* (New Haven, Conn.: Yale University Press, 1974); cp. also E. Auerbach, *Mimesis* (Garden City, N.Y.: Anchor/Doubleday & Co., 1953), pp. 5–20.

9. However, we do have the translation of Enoch (Gen. 5:24).

10. E. Auerbach, *Mimesis,* p. 6, ventures the opinion: "The concept of God held by the Jews is less a cause than a symptom of their manner of comprehending and representing things." This is an unlikely thesis, and Auerbach himself says the opposite later (p. 19): "The sublime influence of God here reaches so deeply into the everyday that the two realms of the sublime and the everyday are not only actually unseparated but basically inseparable."

11. There are occasional glimpses into the heavenly realm in the psalms, prophetic calls, and of course the rather polytheistic Job 1—2, but biblical literature as a whole shows a reticence toward speaking of other dimensions.

achieve his identity in an ideal world. It is the broken, sinful and unjust world of our common experience that the biblical God must enter and transform. The same insistence that God intervene to heal real illness and rectify real injustice appears in the psalms of lament.

Beginning with the exodus, specific historical events from the nation's past become the subject of narration. These accounts are not critically accurate history, at least not until the history of David, but actual events do back up the story. The truth claims of the narratives depend upon their essential historicity, for the events purport to be history making, i.e., decisive modifications of the course of human history. If the accounts were fictional, we would be forced to admit that Yahweh achieved his identity in an ideal world.[12]

If the exodus narrative is granted a historical basis, we can say that the event in which Yahweh was recognized is a constituent of his identity and the identities of those who interact with him. The event was not, that is, merely the occasion for recognition, but a constituent feature of the one recognized: Yahweh is henceforth the God who brought Israel out of Egypt. Likewise, the people who benefit from the event derive their identity from the story. The biblical narrative, thus, has something of the character of autobiographical testimony.[13]

To summarize, the action of the biblical narrative takes place in historical time and space, between God and human personae. The narrative becomes progressively historylike until it becomes dramatized history. At this point, the story becomes the testimony of the participants in the story and of the community which derives its identity from it.

ROLES IN THE ACTION

In this section I will endeavor to substantiate the thesis that the action in which Yahweh participates involves a genuine interaction

---

12. Contrast the view of Thomas L. Thompson, *The Historicity of the Patriarchal Narratives*, BZAW 133 (Berlin: Walter de Gruyter, 1974), p. 328: "The expression of (Israel's) faith finds its condensation in an historical form which sees the past as promise. But this expression is not itself a writing of history, nor is it really about the past, but it is about the present hope."

13. If one is willing to grant the possibility of a *national* autobiography, which of course means that authors who did not themselves experience the events reproduce the national memory.

between a plurality of parties. In the course of the argument, we will examine the allocation of roles. By role, I mean the part played by a person or group in relation to others and to the course of events. A role includes what a party suffers or undergoes as well as what it actively contributes to the action.

A party's role in an action is a conjunction of its identity and of the action in which it participates. On the one hand, a role must be consistent with the character of an individual or the make-up of a group. On the other, a role is the function of social interaction, giving each participant a niche in the overall web of action. The common expression, "thrust into a role," exemplifies the coercive quality of social context.

The identity of Yahweh provides the framework for the role he plays in the actions depicted in biblical literature. The very fact that he, and he alone, is God posits his relatedness to all human personae. He is God for all other parties and must relate to each in ways that are consistent with this role and with his character. In addition, because he is God, he is what might be called the "final court of appeal" in all conflicts and couplings between parties.

The particular action determines the actual relations between parties within this framework. For heuristic purposes, I use the classical typology of roles: protagonist, antagonist, and supporting roles. These terms suggest the interrelations between parties as well as the dramatic standing of each. The protagonist is at the center of the action, while the antagonist opposes the purposes of the protagonist. Supporting roles may actually support one of the two competing parties or contribute to the action from a neutral stance. Yahweh can, according to the action, appear in any one of these roles.

To substantiate and fill in this general description, we will briefly examine some texts. For a change of pace, I have chosen to look at psalms of lamentation. Doing so will broaden the textual basis of the book's argument. In addition, we have at hand form critical studies that break down the form according to parties. Thus, the analysis has been accomplished for us on a category-wide basis. All we will need to do is review the analysis and correlate it with the classical typology of roles.

The psalm of lamentation falls under our expression "histrionic utterance." A lament is an existential utterance arising out of personal or national crisis. Not only is it a cry of pain, it is also an active attempt to overcome the alienation of God and to procure his deliverance. We might call it the words of one party of a drama.[14]

The laments of the Psalter can be divided according to whether the supplicant is an individual or the community. The primary components of these laments are complaint and request. These components are usually supplemented by confession of trust and promise of praise.

C. Westermann has argued persuasively that the complaint (*Klage*) falls into three parts: the accusation of God, the complaint about the speaker's suffering and humiliation, and the complaint about the enemies.[15] To take just one example from an individual lament:

> How long, Yahweh, will you forget me forever?
>   How long will you hide your face from me?
> How long must I bear pain in my soul,
>   sorrow in my heart all day long?
> How long shall my enemy be exalted over me?
> (auth. trans. from Hebrew, Ps. 13:2–3, RSV vv. 1–2)

The first bicolon addresses accusing or rebuking questions to God regarding his behavior, the second complains of the supplicant's own suffering, and the concluding stich bemoans the supplicant's humiliation and vulnerability before an enemy.

The tripartite structure of the complaint corresponds to the three parties involved in the situation: God, the supplicant and the supplicant's human counterparts. The act of lamentation is, thus, a *trans*action between three parties. The request follows suit, seeking God's favor and his intervention to save the supplicant and overthrow or disappoint the enemies.[16]

The speaker (or speakers) of the lament is comparable to the protagonist of a narrative. He (or they) has undergone the suffering which provoked the lament and initiates the action to bring the

---

14. This designation is confirmed by the frequent citation of lamentation in the narrative portions of Scripture, e.g., Exod. 5:22–23.

15. "Struktur und Geschichte der Klage im A.T.," in *Forschung am alten Testament*, TBü 24 (München: Chr. Kaiser, 1964), pp. 269–90.

16. C. Westermann, The *Praise of God in the Psalms* (Richmond, Va.: John Knox Press, 1965), pp. 54, 69.

situation to a favorable resolution. God's answer is directed to the supplicant and his intervention turns the fate of the supplicant and leads to a restored relationship.

It is not so easy to identify the antagonist of the lament. In the *communal* lament, the enemy is an actual hostile military force that has brought the people to their knees (e.g., Pss. 44:11b, 14–15; 74:4–8, 10, 18, 22, 23; 79:1–3, 7, 10; 80:13b–14; 89:43–44). If a narrative were to be written of the events that transpired leading to the lamented distress, it would present this enemy as the antagonist of the people. However, the communal lament is strikingly God-centered. It is Yahweh who is accused for the actual disaster and for antagonism toward his people. The earliest communal laments were formulated entirely as accusations against God, and this member continues to overshadow the others in the classical communal lament of the Psalter.[17] Hence, we would have to say that God plays the role of antagonist in the communal lament and the enemy plays the supporting role of instrument and/or interested bystander.

The very nature of communal lamentation and supplication makes God a very special sort of antagonist. The speakers are bold to approach him and to seek to change him from antagonist to deliverer. His antagonism is, as it were, a temporary aberration from past and future favor toward his people.[18] Even in the present, his willingness to hear the cries of his people stands in tension with the experience of divine wrath. The prayer of the community seeks to reestablish communication and to dispel the conflict between them.

The enemy plays a much more prominent role in the vast bulk of *individual* laments and could more easily be identified as the antagonist.[19] In agreement with such an identification is the muteness of accusation against God in most individual laments. Against the identification, however, is the fact that the enemies of the individual are not (as they are in the communal lament) the causes of the dis-

17. Cf. Westermann, "Struktur und Geschichte der Klage im A.T.," pp. 275–77, 292–95.
18. "For his anger is but a moment, and his favor is for a lifetime" (Ps. 30:5).
19. Cf. Westermann, "Struktur und Geschichte der Klage im A.T.," pp. 282–83, 285–89.

tress. Rather, they are neighbors and contemporaries who threaten the supplicant, take advantage of his misfortune, taunt him or speak ill behind his back. Thus, I would say that the enemies of the individual do not represent the real antagonists of the supplicant, but something of a foil and perhaps the objects of deflected anger and fear.

The real antagonist of the individual lament is the same as that of the communal lament: God. It is God who has brought the distress upon the supplicant and who ignores his cries for mercy. The fact is openly admitted in recounting praises from after the time of deliverance, i.e., Ps. 30:6–7:

> As for me, I said in my prosperity,
>   "I shall never be moved."
> . . . .
> thou didst hide thy face,
>   I was dismayed.

A select group of individual laments contain strong accusations against God (Psalms 5, 13, 22, 35, 38, 42, 88, 102).[20] Psalm 88 (as translated by the author from Hebrew) in particular is dominated by this component: "You have put me in the depths of the Pit . . ." (v. 7, also v. 11); "Your wrath lies heavily upon me . . ." (v. 8, also v. 17); "You have caused my companions . . ." (v. 9, also v. 19); "Every day I call upon you . . ." (v. 10); "Yahweh, why do you cast me off?" (v. 15). God is clearly this supplicant's antagonist and he alone can reverse his descent into the land of the dead.

To summarize, Yahweh participates in actions in which there is genuine interaction. The framework of his role is set by his identity. This identity dictates that he be the God of all human participants and the final court of appeals of all interactions. The particular action conditions whether he is protagonist, antagonist or in a supporting role. The psalms of lamentation place him in the role of antagonist over against the supplicant as protagonist. He is a unique sort of antagonist, though, for the supplicant seeks to transform him into the deliverer he was hitherto. The interaction is not limited to

20. Ibid., p. 280.

the God-supplicant relation, for the enemies are always present as a third party.

THE RESOLUTION OF THE ACTION

The term "resolution" used in the title of this section derives from Claus Westermann's form critical definition of narrative. The key words of his definition are *"Lösung der Spannung."*[21] "Resolution" is an appropriately general translation of *Lösung*. The word *Spannung* can be translated by words like "tension," "stress," or "strain." This term characterizes the situation that provokes people to act. The common English expression "tense situation" comes to mind.

A course of events issues from the acts of the protagonist, the resistance of the antagonist, the complications created by third parties, and the effect of the natural environment. The course of events is not random, but teleological: it moves toward the resolution of the original tension.[22] If there were no resolution, the story would continue, for the causes of the original acts would continue.[23]

As one of the participants in the action, Yahweh constitutes a factor in the tense situation and his acts contribute to its resolution. When he is in the role of protagonist or antagonist, he himself is one of the poles of tension. When he is a third party, the chief tension is between other parties and his role is that of an adjudicator.

The attributes that Yahweh possesses by virtue of his exclusive deity decisively affect his contribution. As the one of exemplary moral character, whatever he wills is right. This does not mean that humans cannot protest his actions (the laments are testimony to the right to protest), but they appeal to him precisely as the source of justice (cf. Jer. 12:1). In addition, as the one participant in the

---

21. "Arten der Erzählung in der Genesis," *Forschung am A.T.,* p. 19.
22. Cf. Tom Driver, *The Sense of History in Greek and Shakespearean Tragedy* (New York and London: Columbia University Press, 1960), p. 78: "It might be said that action is (in the root meaning) the 'intension' of the events—that quality in them which puts them, as it were, into tension, and gives them a 'tendency' to a certain outcome."
23. When a story comes to an end, some sort of resolution has occurred. The Leader may not believe that the resolution was satisfactory, but that is another question.

situation with the power and intelligence to accomplish whatever he purposes, the resolution must conform to his will and be appropriated by the other parties as a judgment on their actions.

With such formal principles structuring the interaction between Yahweh and his creatures, one might expect the resolutions of biblical actions to be arbitrary and unrealistic. This is not the case. The biblical God is not—with a few exceptions—depicted as a *deus ex machina* who makes things right by means of arbitrary interventions. First, he is an explicit or implicit party to the action from beginning to end, so his action is not unexpected. Second, his acts are suitable to the dramatic sequence, and the resolution follows inevitably from the entire course of events.

To confirm and fill in this description, I will offer an exposition of the poetic drama of Job. I have selected this text because it dovetails superbly with the psalms of lamentation. In addition, it exemplifies the divine resolution of an action with a formal purity impossible to historical and historylike accounts.

There is a wide range of opinion as to what material in the book of Job is original and whether the interpreter should expound the original in isolation from the rest.[24] I will expound what I take to be the original poetic drama because it exhibits a coherent dramatic structure, while the secondary material and textual dislocations disturb this structure.

The drama falls into two acts. Act one is the dialogue between Job and his three companions before God (chapters 3—27). The dialogue begins with Job's curse of his existence, followed by several cycles of exchanges (Friend 1–Job–Friend 2–Job– . . .). The first two cycles are dramatically coherent and subtly sequential. Cycle three should end with the initial exchange (chapters 22 and 23), for Eliphaz charges Job with being one of the wicked and impious, so Job can no longer talk with them.[25] Act two consists of a long lamentation of Job that concludes with a challenge to God to examine Job's life, which is followed directly by two addresses of

---

24. Cf. Brevard Childs, *Introduction to the Old Testament as Scripture* (Philadelphia: Fortress Press, 1979), pp. 528–43.
25. Cf. 27:5–6, which I would insert in place of the limp 23:2.

Yahweh and responses of Job (chapters 29—31, 38:1—42:6, excising 40:15–24, 41:12–34).[26]

The book of Job has rightly been called a *dramatized lament*.[27] Job is the supplicant, his three companions the enemies. These three visit Job with the intention of comforting and edifying him, but they end up being his persecutors. They exemplify a piety (presumably the orthodoxy of the author's day) that took suffering as an occasion for self-humiliation and self-accusation in the hope of obtaining God's mercy. Their piety has the theological backing of three doctrines: the righteousness of God, the imperfection of all humanity, and the law of retribution. Job refuses to conform to the prescribed piety and finally (chapters 21, 24) challenges its theological backing. He seems to have initially expected his companions to act as his witnesses, but their persecution drives him to seek their silence.

Job's real antagonist is God. His language is replete with images depicting Yahweh as enemy (e.g., 6:4; 7:12; 16:9–14; 19:7–12). In the first cycle, he addresses God vehemently in the language of accusation and challenge. Above all, he wants to discover the grounds of God's condemnation and to be allowed the chance to clear himself. The climax of these addresses occurs in 13:23, when he asks God:

> How great are my iniquities and sins?
> Expose my offense and my sin before me.
> (auth. trans.)

When he receives no answer, he loses his capacity to address God and stumbles toward the hope that his own death will provoke an inquiry which will clear his name and bring reconciliation with the God who can no longer be approached (16:18–21; 19:23–27).[28]

During the dialogue and Job's final lament, God is present in

---

26. My position follows C. Westermann, *Der Aufbau des Buches Hiob*, BHT 23 (Tübingen: J. C. B. Mohr [Paul Siebeck], 1956); ET: *The Structure of the Book of Job: A Form-Critical Analysis*, trans. Charles A. Muenchow (Philadelphia: Fortress Press, 1981).

27. A. Bentzen, *Introduction to the Old Testament*, vol. 2 (Kopenhagen, 1952), p. 182.

28. For this entire paragraph, see my "Job's Address of God," *ZAW* 91/2 (1979), pp. 268–82.

Job's accusations, wishes and third-person descriptions. His is a sinister presence, an intimidating silence. It is the breaking of his silence and the silencing of Job's accusations that resolves the drama. The fact that Yahweh answers is quite as important as what he says.[29] Job says as much in his final confession:

> I had heard of You by the report of the ear,
>   but now my eye has seen You (42:5).
>   (auth. trans.)

The encounter with Yahweh has itself made the difference for Job. Another of his statements develops this point further:

> Now I know that you can do anything,
> and nothing you purpose can be thwarted (42:2).
>   (auth. trans.)

The evidence for this is not only the deeds alluded to in Yahweh's address, but also his decisive resolution of this very action by breaking silence.

One might ask, however, whether what Yahweh says in his addresses really answers the questions posed in the dialogue. Perhaps Yahweh has shifted the ground of the discussion, say by replacing guilt with finitude. If the drama were really a debate over the causes of suffering and the justice of God, one might indeed construe Yahweh's answer as a non sequitur. If one takes it as a dramatized lament, however, the answer is surprising but infinitely satisfying. First, Yahweh accepts the judicial contest proposed by Job and simply exercises his right of cross-examination. Second, he directly disputes both Job's and his companions' correlation of divine justice with the question of guilt or innocence for suffering (40:8). Third, his questions introduce no new knowledge into the drama, but reflect what Job and his companions have said of God all along.[30] It is a sign of the dramatic perfection of the drama that Yahweh quotes back to Job what he has already acknowledged.

It is commonly inferred that the distancing, censorious tone of Yahweh's addresses means that he repudiates Job's questioning, prob-

---

29. To substantiate this idea further, try to imagine the drama without Yahweh's answer; it would sound like a hopeless lament (e.g., Psalm 88).
30. Observed by Westermann, *Der Aufbau des Buches Hiob*, pp. 84f.

ably as an example of human pride. Congruent with this interpretation is the customary translation of 42:3b, 6: "I spoke of things I did not know. . . . Therefore I recant and repent on dust and ashes." It is dramatically necessary that Job show remorse for what he said if Yahweh has condemned it. Job's response must be appropriate to Yahweh's resolution, or he would be condemned.[31]

I have argued elsewhere[32] that 42:3b, 6 can be translated differently: "Therefore I declare—though I do not understand!— wonders beyond me—though I do not comprehend! . . . Therefore I repudiate and foreswear dust and ashes." According to this rendering, Job now joyously confesses Yahweh's mysterious, yet saving wonders and ceases his mourning and lamentation. This assumes that Yahweh's questions were meant to transform Job's accusing acknowledgment to spontaneous praise, but not to condemn what he said earlier. This would provide a more satisfying conclusion to the action of the dialogue. The dialogue elicits our sympathy for and identification with Job, and the resolution should confirm his integrity.

In summary, the poetic drama of Job exhibits the participation of Yahweh in an action which he resolves by addresses appropriate to the action. It is a vivid example of the artistic principles to which the authors of Scripture adhered in their rendering of Yahweh's enactment of his identity.

SUMMATION

On the surface, the subjects covered in this chapter might appear disparate, but from the end point we can see their logical sequence. First, we described the concept of action, which forms the basis of Part Two. The remainder of the chapter examined the interaction of God and his creatures. We identified the personae with whom he interacts, humans, and the stage, the horizon of history. Next, we argued for the constitutive quality of the interaction for Yahweh's identity by showing that he appears in definable roles. Finally, we reflected on the resolution of an action and the artistic principles in depicting Yahweh's contribution.

31. For this reason, I find quite implausible J. B. Curtis' view that Job continues in his defiance, argued in "On Job's Response to Yahweh," *JBL* 98/4 (1979):497–511.

32. ' Short Note: The Translation of Job XLII 6," *VT* 26/3 (1976):369–71.

CHAPTER 5

The Action
of God

Now that we have located Yahweh within a dramatic context, it is time to turn to that aspect of action which is predicated of a subject. To interact, one must act. For Yahweh to play a role in an action and to contribute to its resolution, he must say and do things that exert a sovereign influence on the other participants and on the course of events. It is this saying and doing that will concern us in this and the next chapter.

It would be belaboring the obvious to devote our efforts to demonstrating that Yahweh is depicted as acting. Any reader of the Old Testament notices it immediately. If anyone happens to miss its importance, biblical theologians will happily point that out. Indeed, the "acts of God in history" was the slogan under which many of us marched not too long ago. The title of G. E. Wright's manifesto, *The God Who Acts,*[1] declared our position.

I am now convinced that we should avoid elevating the conceptual abstraction, God acts in history, into a theologumenon. It is relatively accurate as a statement about the biblical rendering of God, but it should not be isolated from the other components of the rendering and the specific body of literature which depicts his action. To draw from Scripture a proposition to the effect that there exists a God who acts in history distorts the language.

Our task is to show that depiction of Yahweh as acting employs the art of representation. The authors of this literature sought to convince their audience that this or that event had Yahweh as its

---

1. SBT 8 (London: SCM Press, 1952).

author. To accomplish this, they evoked the subjective experience of the divine persona and the objective appearance of his act.

The biblical authors were not confronted with the necessity of showing that deity intervened[2] in human affairs. They shared and cultivated a common ancient Near Eastern world view that allowed for divine interventions. Within this cultural milieu, it was taken for granted that events had divine agents. Some events, like plagues, earthquakes and sudden, unexpected turns of fortune, were ascribed to direct divine intervention, while others, like wars, social change and fateful decisions were believed to be mediated acts of deity. It was also taken for granted that such interventions manifested motive, deliberation and purpose. That is, an occurrence ascribed to divine agency was believed to be expressive of the deity's emotional state (anger, pleasure, etc.) and to be calculated to accomplish the deity's intention (to punish, reward, save, etc.).[3]

It was the duty of the author to embody these assumptions in narrative, prophecy, law, or psalm. One had to tell stories, for example, in which divine interventions could be recognized as such by the audience. At his or her disposal was a cultural tradition that associated certain occurrences or concatenations of events with deity. To reinforce recognition, the humans in the account could be depicted as responding to the occurrences as divine interventions. When humans responded appropriately, the divine act would be given the weight due it, i.e., it would influence the subsequent course of events. If they did not respond appropriately, the story itself would turn on their foolishness and impiety.

Biblical authors not only had to convince their audience of divine interventions, but also to ascribe all such interventions to one and the same persona. This means that all depictions of divine interventions had to be consistent with the one who possessed divine

2. The expression "divine intervention" is well established in our theological vocabulary for occurrences within human history that are caused by God. Intervention is a somewhat unfortunate word, for it suggests that natural processes and human affairs are closed systems occasionally punctured by an alien cause. The biblical God is far too active in the affairs of his creatures to be called an outsider. On the other hand, the expression rightly suggests that the action of God is particular and recognizable.

3. See B. Albrektson, *History and the Gods,* Coniectanea Biblica, OT Series 1 (Lund: C. W. K. Gleerup, 1967).

attributes to an exclusive degree and who manifested distinctive, recognizable personal traits in the story of his deeds. In other words, each rendering of a divine intervention had to take the entire Yahwistic tradition into account and demonstrate that it was a fitting extension of that tradition. If the author succeeded, the act depicted became a once-and-for-all enactment of Yahweh's identity. Henceforth he would be known as the one who did thus and so in the course of his many and various deeds.

In the following sections, we will isolate and describe components of the representation of Yahweh's action. Under the heading "imagery and plotting" we will survey the occurrences and concatenations of events that are ascribed to Yahweh and their placement in the story line. Under the rubric "motivation, deliberation and purpose" we will endeavor to show that divine interventions are portrayed as the work of a subject.

The chapter's textual focus will be a select group of narratives from Genesis and Exodus. The study of these narratives will be supplemented by some general observations on classical prophecy.

THE IMAGERY AND PLOTTING OF DIVINE INTERVENTION

The word "imagery" was chosen to suggest the literary function of the depictions of God's interventions in human affairs. It is our contention that the events ascribed to divine agency can be interpreted as serving artistic purposes. In particular, we shall argue that such events establish God's active presence and show how he exerted a decisive influence on the course of events.

By "plotting" we mean the selection and arrangement of actions and occurrences to tell a story. An author selects the incidents that contribute to the action he or she seeks to represent, arranges them sequentially and structures each internally to embody and contribute to the development of this action. Our interest is with the placement and structuring of the accounts of divine intervention.

First, we need to consider the artistic function of the depiction of occurrences ascribed to divine authorship. For a human character, an author can evoke the "feel" of an action to convince the audience that the character did what was attributed to him or her. The depiction of Yahweh was under severe restraints in this respect, for his ways are mysterious and beyond human comprehension. Only to a very limited extent was the author allowed to describe how God caused something to happen.[4] In the place of this type of depiction, the authors evoked the human perception of the occurrences. Odd, spectacular, catastrophic or uncanny occurrences, for example, gave a prima facie impression of divine origin.

Natural catastrophes—violent storms, droughts, plagues, pestilence—were generally considered to be of divine origin in Israel and in the ancient world in general. In fact, this understanding is still preserved in our English expression "act of God." When a biblical narrator depicted a story with an "act of God," there was little question in the audience's mind as to its divine origin. The question for both the characters of the story and the audience was: Why has God done this? In the story of Abraham's deception of the Egyptians respecting Sarah's marital status (Gen. 12:10–19, also 20:1–18), plagues tip off the Egyptian king that he is violating divine law and he acts immediately to remedy the situation. The story does not explain how he knew that Sarah was the cause of divine displeasure, but other accounts in Scripture have the ruler seek a revelation of God (e.g., Josh. 7:1ff.; 2 Sam. 21:1ff.). Since this type of "act of God" prima facie suggests divine displeasure, one would expect such a revelation to identify the cause.

The divine intervention in this story plays a significant part in resolving the action favorably, but it would be a mistake to say that the story was told to highlight the intervention. The background tension of the story is the vulnerability of foreigners in a strange land, particularly if they have something or someone desirable. The patriarch tries to neutralize the danger, but he actually aggravates it. Losing Sarah to the royal harem is hardly what he wanted! The divine intervention is able to undo Abraham's mistake, but it does not solve the underlying problem. The vulnerability of foreigners is "solved" by their expulsion![5] Thus, the account is of human conflict and resolution which a divine intervention deflects from tragic consequences.

The exodus account (Exodus 1—15) portrays a wide variety of

---

4. This does not mean that the authors could not depict the natural means, but that they could not describe how God manipulates this means.
5. Gen. 20:9–18 has a much happier conclusion.

divine interventions. Two stand out in the account and later memory: the plagues and the drowning of the Egyptian army. The plagues are "acts of God," much like the Genesis account just examined. However, they stand out in number and for their dramatic structure. They are announced beforehand to the pharaoh so that he will recognize their author and purpose when they occur. The pharaoh's resistance to the divine commands associated with the plagues is quite at variance with the pharaoh of Abraham's time, who prudently heeds the divine warning. The divine interventions in the exodus account are thus no longer warnings, but rather moves in a power struggle. On the one hand, they demonstrate Yahweh's power ("signs and wonders"); on the other, the pharaoh's stubbornness.

The deliverance of the escaping slaves by drowning the Egyptian army at the Sea of Reeds is a somewhat different sort of divine intervention. First, it is an occurrence which itself effects salvation. It is not a warning or an application of pressure to prompt humans to comply with the divine will, but the direct creation of the desired outcome.

Second, the imagery of the divine intervention does not draw upon commonly experienced and recognized acts of God. Rather, the act is unique and therefore revelatory of the unique power and moral character of the divine actor: "Fear not, stand firm and see the salvation of the Lord, which we will work for you today . . ." (Exod. 14:13 J). "I will get glory over Pharaoh and all his host . . . and the Egyptians shall know that I am the Lord . . ." (14:17–18 P). Such concentration on the revelatory force of this particular divine intervention serves to identify Yahweh in his uniqueness and to substantiate his claim to be the author of all interventions.

Third, the authors exhibit a far greater curiosity toward the details of the event than usual. P accentuates the miraculous character of the event, probably to establish beyond doubt its authorship by Yahweh.[6] Who could attribute the parting of the sea to natural causes? J appears to want to identify the means employed by Yahweh.[7] A wind blows the water back and then ceases, and the

---

6. To P belong: 14:1–4, 8–9, 10, 15–18, 21c–23, 26–27a, 28–29.
7. Cf. M. Noth, *Exodus* (Philadelphia: Westminster Press, 1962), pp. 115–20.

Egyptians are terrorized by Yahweh and rush (?) into the returning water (14:19b–20, 21ab, 24–25, 30–31). One suspects that J was writing for a sophisticated audience for whom a miracle would be less believable than an intervention through recognizable means. Both authors thus seek to establish the credibility of Yahweh's intervention, though with opposite concerns and imagery.

The plot of the exodus narrative involves divine interventions throughout. The crisis develops without overt intervention, but even it has Yahweh's hidden action—the multiplication of the people—at its basis. The call of Moses inaugurates the actual struggle for liberation. Moses' initial negotiations with the pharaoh (Exodus 5) begin the struggle between Yahweh, the protagonist, and the pharaoh, his antagonist. The contest between them builds from plague to plague, and the pharaoh's resistance is finally cracked by the slaughter of the firstborn. However, in one last, absurd act of defiance he tries to stop the departing slaves and brings disaster upon himself and his people. The promise that ignited the struggle has been fulfilled.

In the exodus narrative, divine interventions so dominate and penetrate the course of events that they become a series which makes up one comprehensive intervention. Once the promise has been issued to Moses, practically every scene turns upon some intervention and each intervention builds upon previous ones. We can say that Yahweh proceeds step-by-step to procure the freedom of his people. Few scriptural narratives are so dominated and structured by divine intervention. It is no accident that the exodus became the fulcrum of Yahwistic tradition.

One often thinks of divine interventions in terms of spectacular events like the examples just studied, but the term can also be applied to the hidden work of divine providence. The Joseph novella (Genesis 37, 39—50) provides a good example. Dreams, which were automatically ascribed to supernatural sources in ancient society, are the only specific occurrences ascribed to Yahweh in the story. Otherwise, God's action is hidden in the twist of fate that transformed Joseph's brothers' ill-will into good for all: "You meant evil against me [Joseph]; but God meant it for good, to bring it about that many people should be kept alive, as they are today" (Gen. 50:20; cf. 45:7–8). The ironies and accidents that shape the course of history and bring unintended consequences out of human purposes were occurrences in which the ancients—particularly the sophisticated—found evidence of divine activity.

Recognition of hidden divine intervention is essential to its depiction. It is only when Joseph recognizes God's intervention in the course of his life that we the readers recognize it. The moment of recognition is itself an epiphany that contributes to the resolution of the action (enticing Jacob to Egypt in Gen. 45:9–11, reconciling the brothers in chapter 50). The reader is provoked to review the course of events from this new perspective.

To conclude this analysis of the imagery and plotting of divine intervention, let us turn from the past interventions of Yahweh to the announcement of a future one. The classical prophets were called to persuade their audience to recognize that Yahweh was about to intervene. In distinction from the narrators, these prophets had to establish that Yahweh's coming intervention was not simply one in a series, but rather was decisive and in some sense final. Amos recites a series of divine interventions—mostly "acts of God"—that have failed to turn Israel around (4:4–11), so the series will soon come to a climax:

> Therefore, thus I will do to you, O Israel;
> because I will do this to you,
> prepare to meet your God, O Israel!
>   (4:12)

The indefinite allusion to what Yahweh is about to do was probably supplemented by a threatening gesture. Soon Israel must meet its destiny, confront its God once and for all. The coming encounter would be the end of the people of Yahweh, the end of election, the end of violence and injustice (Amos 8:1ff.; 9:1ff.; etc.). If there is to be a new beginning, it must involve a decisive break with the past.[8]

The coming intervention announced by the classical prophets has, one might say, the force of all divine interventions of the past taken collectively. This allowed the prophets to draw upon the whole range of imagery associated with past interventions and prompted the cre-

---

8. See chapter 7, Eschatology.

ation of new imagery. The chief image was the attack and conquest of foreign powers.[9] They also, however, drew upon lament, judicial process, epiphany, primal creation, domestic conflict, farming practices, and the attack of wild beasts to evoke the sense of impending doom and possible renewal. Some of these recalled past encounters and heightened the sense of climax. Others were not associated with past interventions and relied upon their dramatic cogency to evoke the coming intervention.

To summarize, the depictions of divine interventions in narrative and prophecy serve the artistic purposes of convincing the audience of Yahweh's active presence in human affairs and of showing how he brings human affairs to a satisfactory or appropriate resolution. Although there was a variety of kinds of divine intervention, each in its own way met the need of convincing the audience. The plotting varied according to the type of occurrence and role of recognition, for the divine intervention had to contribute to the course of events according to its intrinsic character and importance. The prophets announced a coming intervention with the force of all divine interventions taken collectively, so they could draw from all actual and potential images of divine intervention to convince their audience that this ultimate intervention was imminent. All our examples identified Yahweh as the author of the occurrence, but some made this of greater consequence (above all, the exodus and the classical prophets) than the others.

THE MOTIVATION, DELIBERATION AND PURPOSE OF DIVINE INTERVENTION

The difference between a human action and the action of a machine is the subjective dimension. A human action involves the operation of consciousness. A depiction of the action of a human requires, as a consequence, the evocation of motive, deliberation or planning, and purpose (the end toward which one acts). To understand and enter into a person's action (to reenact imaginatively),

---

9. B. Albrektson, *History and the Gods,* makes a strong case for a wide diffusion of this idea in the ancient Near East.

the audience must know to what end the person is acting, why the person has chosen this end, and how the things the person does work toward this end.

The biblical authors render Yahweh as conscious and self-conscious, and hence depicted his action as motivated, deliberate and purposeful. In the following paragraphs, we will examine briefly this aspect of their representation of divine interventions. We will avoid repeating the analysis of God's inner dialogue (chapter 1), expecting the reader to relate those conclusions to the present subject of discussion.

The authors of biblical narrative establish the motivation and purposefulness of divine interventions in several ways. Where a tradition existed that suggested the meaning of a given type of intervention, the author could simply assume this meaning. For obvious reasons, a plague or a violent storm suggested divine displeasure. In Gen. 12:17, the plague is taken as a warning by the pharaoh that he is about to commit an offense. The narrative assumes that adultery is an offense which would arouse divine displeasure, no matter who the parties were. The fact that it is Sarah, the matriarch designate of the people of God, adds a further dimension of urgency, for Yahweh is uniquely committed to the protection and fulfillment of this couple. The warning was an act of justice toward the pharaoh, keeping him from violating the divine order inadvertently.

When the action of a story is inaugurated by Yahweh's promise, the interventions that follow are recognized as fulfillment. They serve the purpose of bringing the promised situation to realization. In the exodus narrative, the plagues bear a special meaning because of the promise of liberation. They are to break the pharaoh's resistance and procure Israel's release.[10] This purpose is stated explicitly to the pharaoh when a plague is announced.

Classical prophecy of judgment inverts the relation of purpose and motivation to intervention. The prophet seeks to convince his audience that Yahweh is about to intervene by showing that he had good reason to. Yahweh is compelled to act by the contradiction between his will and his people's behavior. Form critics have rightly termed

10. They have, of course, a reflexive purpose as well: to show forth Yahweh's power.

the accusations leveled against the addressee the "grounds" for the intervention.[11] The offenses and systematic corruption of the people necessitate a divine response, e.g., "Shall I not punish them for these things, says the Lord; and shall I not avenge myself on a nation such as this?" (Jer. 5:9). Punishment is required for their guilt, vengeance is required for betrayal and treachery. Such deeds must have consequences for the perpetrators.[12] God must vindicate his law and honor.

The "contrast motif"[13] draws out the contradiction between Yahweh's will and the human situation by juxtaposing his grace and his people's response, e.g., "When I fed them to the full, they committed adultery and trooped to the houses of harlots" (Jer. 5:7b). The gracious deeds of Yahweh in the past had, by implication, the purpose of creating a faithful community, but the actual result was the opposite. The contradiction requires resolution.

As to purpose in God's intervention, the divine judgment announced by the prophets cannot be fully comprehended under the category of punishment.[14] It is not simply a matter of penalties imposed for overt offenses or consequences for deeds, though it is that. Statements like the following suggest something more: "How can I pardon you? Your children have forsaken me, and have sworn by those who are no gods" (Jer. 5:7a). The betrayal could in fact be pardoned if the type of behavior had ceased. The problem is that the community has a history of betrayal from which it cannot free itself. This history, with its own irresistible and irreversible momentum, encompassing the coming generation as it assumes its place in the sequence of generations, requires drastic measures: it must be brought to an end.

11. C. Westermann, *Basic Forms of Prophetic Speech* (Philadelphia: Westminster Press, 1967), pp. 97, 142ff., 170ff.
12. Cf., with reservation, K. Koch, "Gibt es ein Vergeltungsdogma im Alten Testament?" in *ZTK* 52 (1955):1–42; also J. C. Gammie, "The Theology of Retribution in the Book of Deuteronomy," *CBQ* 32/1 (1970):1–12.
13. C. Westermann, *Basic Forms of Prophetic Speech*, pp. 182–85.
14. T. Frymer-Kensky, "The Atrahasis Epic and Its Significance for Our Understanding of Genesis 1–9," *BA* 40/4 (1977):147–55, argues against the idea that the flood was punishment for specific offenses; rather it suggests that the flood was a purgation of the land in preparation for the institution of law to counter-balance the human impulse to evil. The prophets obviously announced divine punishment, but this other purpose may also be seen.

To summarize, the authors of biblical narrative render divine interventions as the motivated and purposeful action of a subject. This subjective dimension may be obvious from the form of the intervention and the story itself, so left implicit. On the other hand, the statement of motivated purpose may prepare for the intervention. The prophets worked from motive and purpose to divine intervention. The contradiction between Yahweh's will and his people's behavior calls for punishment and the breaking of the momentum of history.

SUMMATION AND THEOLOGICAL REFLECTION

This chapter was devoted to the examination of the artistic means by which Yahweh is presented to the reader of the Old Testament as acting in human affairs. This representation was built upon the cultural assumption of the ancient Near East that certain occurrences and concatenations of events were attributable to divine agency. The biblical authors had the task of ascribing all divine interventions to Yahweh.

The representation of Yahweh's intervention was broken down into two components. First, we examined the events selected and rendered as Yahweh's acts and the ways these events were arranged within the course of the story. The narrators selected and arranged interventions that would be convincing and important for the action. The classical prophets announced a decisive intervention of God and drew on the full arsenal of imagery capable of evoking the force of the coming action. Second, we described the subjective aspect of divine interventions. The narrators used a variety of means to suggest that a divine intervention manifested motivation and served a purpose. The classical prophets expended great effort convincing their audience that the announced intervention was well motivated and purposeful.

The modern reader of Scripture does not share the ancient assumptions about divine interventions. Nature and history are interpreted in terms of finite causes only. Our natural and social sciences exclude divine agency from the accounts of the processes studied. Although we still have the expression "act of God," we no longer look for the cause of divine displeasure when we experience one. An uncanny turn of events is more likely to be ascribed to "luck" than to God.

This cultural gap may make the modern reader of Scripture skeptical of its depiction of divine interventions. One might say that we have difficulty appreciating the aesthetic sensibility that informs these accounts. Events which for the authors and their audience evoked the sense of divine presence no longer do so for us. What was realism for them seems unrealistic to us. We may feel comfortable with some of the imagery, but it is likely that we will find other parts of it quite foreign and incredible.

The only cure for this dissonance is for the modern reader to suspend his or her sensibility in order to enter the aesthetic sensibility of the biblical world. One must do this to appreciate any work from another historical era.

Once one enters the biblical world, the interventions of Yahweh carry a great power of conviction. We can imagine an act of God exhibiting divine displeasure and prompting us to find the cause, even if we do not do so in our own lives. The story becomes strikingly realistic again, once we allow ourselves to experience the events as they are depicted.

The events ascribed to Yahweh's action are depicted as they were experienced.[15] Israelites recognized his presence in their lives and this recognition entered into their decisions and actions. Scripture would be much less realistic if it portrayed the events of history not as the participants experienced them, but as a modern historian would.

Belief in the reality of the biblical God does not require that we experience events as ancient Israelites did. All that is required is that we be able to suspend our assumptions to encounter the biblical God within the tradition through which he enters human history and to recognize that the same God is active in our world within our sensibilities.

15. I suspect that the Yahwist depicted Yahweh as naively as he did in the early stories of Genesis for a very sophisticated reason: his depiction corresponded to the way he imagined that the human characters would have experienced him.

CHAPTER 6

God's Speaking

During the heyday of the biblical theology movement it was rather common to distinguish between Yahweh's acts and his speaking. Gerhard von Rad set the tone in statements like this: "There is . . . a surprising discord in the answers which the Old Testament gives to the question of the particular way in which this knowledge of God was attained in Israel. At a first glance, two sets of statements seem to be opposed to each other without any interconnection—God revealed himself by means of his words, and God revealed himself by means of his acts."[1] He then proceeds to assert that the acts of Yahweh in history represent a prereflective stage of consciousness, while Yahweh's speaking constitutes a stage of theological reflection.[2]

This dualism of word and deed is quite artificial. Serious reflection would suggest that God's word is a component of his action. James Barr is to the point when he says: "The acts of God are meaningful because they are set within a frame of verbal communication. God tells what he is doing, or tells what he is going to do. . . . A God who acted in history would be a mysterious and superpersonal fate if the action was not linked with this verbal communication."[3] Our study has already confirmed Barr's observation: God's

1. *Old Testament Theology*, vol. 2 (Edinburgh and London: Oliver & Boyd, 1965), p. 358.
2. Ibid., pp. 358–60.
3. *Old and New in Interpretation* (New York: Harper & Row, 1966), pp. 77f.

motivation and purpose are necessary components of the depiction of a divine intervention, and his speaking is a common means of revealing them.

In this chapter, I will endeavor to show that God's speaking not only provides a framework of meaning but also enters into the course of human affairs as a mode of action in its own right. The study falls into two parts. First, the depiction of God's speaking will be categorized as a type of divine intervention. The operative concept for this analysis will be *audition*. The second and more extended part is devoted to describing how God can accomplish something in the very act of speaking.

The textual focus of the chapter is the accounts of theophanies in Genesis and Exodus. The call of Moses will again be given special attention. The central text, however, will be one that has not been expounded hitherto: the covenant making at Sinai.

AUDITIONS

The expression "audition" is the technical term for a human's hearing supernatural voices. Auditions are a common and recurring phenomenon of world religions. The depictions of Yahweh's speaking conform to the general pattern. Israel shared the assumption of its ancient Near Eastern milieu that deity could be manifested visually and orally within the finite world to human beings. When such encounters occurred, they were memorable and were reenacted dramatically to establish the active presence of Yahweh in human affairs.

LITERARY DEPICTION

Within a literary context, an audition is a mode of artistic expression used by authors to evoke the presence of God as an active agent. This type of intervention was so well established in biblical tradition that an author could rely upon its credibility to his or her audience. To be sure, the depiction had to fall within the conventions of portraying auditions, but for that very reason this image of divine intervention was potent and adaptable.

Auditions are closely associated with theophanies. By "theophany" is meant the visual experience of God, supernatural phenomena, or uncanny disruptions in natural phenomena due to God's presence.[4] Not all depictions of auditions involve visual experience, but many do. If one accepts Claus Westermann's distinction between epiphany and theophany, the latter always involve auditions.[5] It might be said that theophany within biblical literature is a way of augmenting an audition to heighten its dramatic force and reinforce the claim that a divine intervention has occurred.

There is a degree of variation and development in the understanding of the relation of theophany and normal consciousness. In the earlier portion of the narrative, God (or his surrogates) is depicted as if he were the object of normal conscious perception. This is true of the primordial history to an extreme degree, but it holds true of theophanies to the patriarchs and to Moses and Israel at Sinai. With the account of the conquest and period of the judges, the *malak-Yahweh* replaces Yahweh himself as the object of perception.[6] The prophetic calls suggest that God is seen in a supernormal state of consciousness and therefore that a theophany is a "vision" of another plane of reality.[7]

Beginning with the patriarchs, the tradition also has theophanic auditions occur in dreams, one type of altered consciousness. Dreams are visual experiences, so auditions that occur in dreams are theophanic. In content, they seem to differ in imagery; they usually contain symbolic figures that are deciphered by a word (e.g., Gen. 28: 12–17; 37:6–11). Since biblical authors lived in a cultural milieu in which dreams were ascribed to supernatural sources, they could rely upon audience acceptance of this image of divine intervention.

Auditions are plotted anywhere in the course of a narrative where other types of divine intervention occur. Auditions in which a pro-

---

4. Examples of each: visual perception of God: Gen. 15:7–21; 18:1–3; Exod. 24:9–11; 33:18–23/34:4–5; supernatural phenomena other than God: Gen. 32:1f.; 32:24ff.; cf. 28:12 (E); uncanny disruptions of nature: Exod. 3:1ff.; 19:16ff.

5. The *Praise of God in the Psalms* (Richmond, Va.: John Knox Press, 1965), pp. 98–101.

6. Cf. C. Westermann, *Basic Forms of Prophetic Speech* (Philadelphia: Westminster Press, 1967), p. 100.

7. Num. 12:6–8 even seems to differentiate prophets from Moses on this basis.

tagonist is called and commissioned to act occur frequently at the outset of an action (e.g., Gen. 12:1-3; Exod. 3:1ff.). They may bring a story to resolution (Gen. 3:14-19; 4:10-12; Exod. 15:25, 26). They occur in the middle of the action as well, warning and instructing human participants as to what they should do (e.g., Gen. 20:3-7; Exod. 5:22—6:1). Like other divine interventions, an audition was plotted according to what it contained and how it was expected to affect the course of events.[8]

Auditions are so integrated into narratives involving interventions of other types that we found no occasion in the last chapter to honor the distinction between act and word. The divine word inaugurates, interprets and resolves actions involving nonverbal interventions. In a word, God's speaking works in tandem with occurrences in nature and history to bring about his purposes.

To Whom?

Aside from the account of the event at Sinai, direct auditions occur only with individuals. The community experiences the auditions through reporting. The individuals who receive them are expected to convey the divine word to the community.

The mediatorial role changes as the biblical narrative progresses. In the Book of Genesis, God speaks directly with the human protagonist. The only mediatorial function is that of a person, namely, a patriarch or matriarch who represents the family before God. With Moses, the narrative begins to limit auditions to select figures with leadership status accruing to them because of the auditions. These persons convey to the people the word received in their auditions. From Moses' time into the period of the monarchy, the mediators also function as political leaders, but after Solomon one hears no longer of leaders receiving auditions. Receiving auditions becomes the special province of the prophets, whose role is primarily one of being spokesman for God.

The account of the theophany and covenant making at Sinai does report that the people as a whole heard the divine declaration of the

---

8. It is noteworthy that a dream plays the same role in Gen. 20:3-7 as the plague does in Gen. 12:17.

decalogue (Exod. 20:1ff.). However, the very same source (E) adumbrates the idea that the people only saw and heard the uncanny disruptions in nature and chose Moses to receive the auditory revelation (20:18–21). What emerges in the extant text is a dialectical, even paradoxical, sequence in which the people hear Yahweh's word and then recruit Moses to convey to them the word that Yahweh has spoken.[9]

To summarize our discussion of auditions, we can say that they conform to our description of divine interventions. They function to establish God's active presence in the narrative. Theophany augments this function. They are plotted anywhere in a story and they work in tandem with nonverbal interventions. Individuals receive them and convey the message to the community. At Sinai, all Israel hears Yahweh's word directly but then asks Moses to convey it to the people.

THE ACTIVE FORCE OF SPEAKING

If the auditions and mediated communication of God are divine interventions, our understanding of their contribution to the course of events will be advanced by applying a theory of speech that accounts for the active force of speaking.[10] In the following paragraphs, just such a theory will be described and then applied to examples from the biblical text.

The philosopher J. L. Austin has developed a theory of speech that highlights the active force of speaking.[11] In addition to the content of a statement, there is the act of speaking itself. What the act adds to the content is *illocutionary* force. All utterances have illocutionary force, but some are constituted by it. These Austin calls

9. This present arrangement is probably not original, but it is certainly interesting and even a bit ironic.

10. Although there are a host of provocative and fruitful approaches to language and the art of communication, it is legitimate to select one that suits the purposes at hand.

11. My discussion is based upon R. W. Jenson, *The Knowledge of Things Hoped For* (New York: Oxford University Press, 1969), pp. 114–18. Austin's own writing on the subject: "Performative Utterances," *Philosophical Papers* (Oxford: Clarendon Press, 1961), pp. 220–29; *How to Do Things with Words* (Cambridge, Mass.: Harvard University Press, 1961).

"performatives." In a performative utterance, the speaker creates in the act of speaking the state of affairs described in it.

The simplest example of a performative utterance is the act of naming. When a person authorized to do so names someone or something, that act causes the person or thing to be so named.

There are other linguistic acts which possess an illocutionary force similar to naming. For example, promises, commands and judicial judgments create facts in the act of speaking. When a person makes a promise, the act of speaking binds the speaker to the stated course of action. A command, if issued by one in authority, binds the addressee to the stated course of action. The verdict of an authorized judge or court establishes innocence and guilt before the law and within the community recognizing that law.

Distinct from the act of speaking is the effect the act has on the hearer. A performative utterance dictates the appropriate response. The act of naming should compel the listener to call the person or thing by its proper name. Promising calls for trusting, commanding calls for obedience, and declaring a verdict calls for acceptance. Of course, it is quite possible for a disparity to arise between the act and the response. An inappropriate response is likely to provoke further action on the part of the speaker to eliminate the disparity, and perhaps this in turn will ignite a power struggle between speaker and hearer.

Austin's theory of language and classification of speech acts provides a conceptual scheme for interpreting God's speaking in biblical literature. By means of it, we can grasp how this God does things with words. In the following two sections we will examine several texts for the illocutionary force of God's speaking.

THE CALL OF MOSES

The call of Moses is the biblical audition *kat' exuchen*. Moses sees a supernatural fire and hears the voice of God. The audition transforms this individual into a mediator who conveys the word received to the people addressed and begins a long life of hearing. The word received prepares for and inaugurates a course of action culminating in the creation of the people of Yahweh.

Yahweh delivers a *promise* and a *command* to Moses and through

Moses to the people. Both of these are illocutionary acts. The promise to deliver Israel from Egyptian slavery binds Yahweh to a course of action. The recipients of the promise can predicate their actions upon this word.

Connected with the promise is a command to Moses. The command is to act as the agent of the promise: "Come, I will send you to Pharaoh that you may bring forth my people, the sons of Israel, out of Egypt" (Exod. 3:10). The promise imposes responsibility upon its recipient to act accordingly and thereby facilitate its fulfillment. For Moses this means taking the role of leader; for the people, obeying Yahweh and his designated agent. The promise is a *trans*action between divine giver and human recipients in which obedient reception becomes a component in the divine action.

To summarize, we see in the call of Moses the performance of two interrelated illocutionary acts. Yahweh binds himself to a course of action and obligates the recipients to act accordingly.[12]

COVENANT MAKING AT SINAI

Covenant making is a verbal action with illocutionary force. The interchange of words defines the relationship between parties and puts it into effect. The covenant-making account of the older Sinaitic tradition (Exodus 19—24, 32—34) has preeminence among the various depictions of acts defining and effecting the relationship between Yahweh and Israel. The patriarchal covenants point forward to it as a climax, and subsequent covenant making renews it.[13] The Sinai account is the logical text to expound if one seeks to grasp what the covenant-making tradition was about.

The older Sinaitic narrative is such a complex tangle of sources and editorial additions that it would be too treacherous to expound the account source by source.[14] However, it would be just as confusing to yield to the extant story line. What seems possible and use-

12. The same double action undoubtedly runs through the promises of Scripture. The prophecy of judgment, on the other hand, involves a declaration of judgment, a more complex performative act, and a more dialectical obligation.
13. By patriarchal covenants are meant the formal promises of Genesis 15 and 17; by covenant renewals: Deuteronomy (particularly chapters 29—31), Joshua 24; also cf. Joshua 23, 1 Samuel 12, 1 Kings 18, 2 Kings 11:17ff.; 23:1ff.
14. I have offered a source division in "The Covenant Code Source," *VT* 27/2 (1977):145–57.

ful is to work from an outline followed by the various component narratives:

1. Sanctification and theophany (19:3-25)
2. Giving of the law (20:1-17; 20:22—23:19; 34:10-28)
3. Ratification of the covenant (24:1-11; 34:29-35)

While there may be small deviations and additional incidents in one account or another, these components are shared by all.

The outline itself exhibits the unique structure of the action: both verbal acts and nonverbal occurrences serve an illocutionary purpose. That is, all words and events serve the purpose of defining and putting into effect the relationship between Yahweh and Israel. As to classification, the acts have a promissory force. They differ from promises that, like the promise of deliverance from Egypt, look toward a specific act. Rather, the promises are of *continuous* activity within an ongoing relationship of reciprocal obligation.

The structure of the relationship created by the action involves Yahweh's authority to command and the concomitant duty of the Israelites to obey. Theophany introduces the sovereign to his subjects. Commandment and law are an exercise of authority by Yahweh over his subjects. Ritual defines the relationship and puts it into effect.

1. Theophanies play a large role in the Sinaitic account.[15] Before the people Yahweh manifests himself visibly in awe-inspiring physical phenomena (Exod. 19:16-19; 20:18-21; 24:17). The seventy elders of Israel are allowed to gaze upon him during a sacred meal (24:9-11). Moses is allowed to view him from the back (33:17—34:28; cf. 24:15-18). The general purpose of these theophanies is to allow the people to meet their God (19:17; also 24:10-11; 33:18-23). This is itself a supreme act of grace (33:19; 24:10-11).

This gracious act of divine self-disclosure simultaneously exemplifies the relationship of sovereign to subject. When the people respond in fear and ask Moses to act as mediator, he assures them: "Do not fear, for God has come to prove you, in order that the fear of him may be before your eyes, that you may not sin" (20:20). Here theophany is subsumed under the establishment of Yahweh's au-

---

15. See K. Kuntz, *The Self-Revelation of God* (Philadelphia: Westminster Press, 1967), pp. 72-103.

thority and Israel's duty to obey him. A few verses later the oral aspect of the theophany is taken as a demonstration of Yahweh's authority to command (20:22). In his theophany to Moses, Yahweh proclaims his gracious nature, a component of which is his enforcement of right (34:7). It is clear, then, that theophany is not a naked encounter with an indeterminate holy presence, but an encounter exemplifying the structure to be created.

2. There are at least three collections of law in the older Sinaitic narrative (20:1–17; 20:22—23:19; 34:10–26). All actualize Yahweh's authority to command Israel by having him exercise it. The relationship of divine sovereignty over Israel is created by being enacted. Israel becomes the community under Yahweh's authority by being addressed in commandments and positive law.

The content of Yahweh's commandments and law corresponds to the formal structure. Each collection has provisions protecting Yahweh's exclusive claim to be Israel's God (20:3–6, 23; 22:20; 23:13; 34:14, 17). The commandments and laws protecting Yahweh's honor (20:7; 22:28) and imposing religious duties (20:8–11; 23:10–19; 34:18–26; also 20:24–26) also give force to the authority structure created by covenant. The commandments and laws governing relationships among the Israelites shape the relationship by bringing human interaction under divine authority and enforcement.[16]

Yahweh's exercise of authority also establishes his judicial position in the community. He is the supreme judge, and human judges exercise their authority as his surrogates and are subject to judgment for the quality of their performance (so 23:1–3, 6–9). When judicial recourse fails, Yahweh himself promises to intervene (e.g., 22:20–26). He is the guarantor of the justice, righteousness and peace of the community under his law.

3. The rituals ratifying the covenant establish the authority of Yahweh and the duty of Israelites to obey him. In Exod. 24:3–8, the ritual involves a twofold reading of the law followed each time by a communal pledge to obey it. The blood rite itself becomes a symbol

---

16. I should voice my opinion that the divine law is exemplary rather than statutory. It articulates the spirit of justice, righteousness and faithfulness by which Yahweh is to be known and Israel to be governed rather than rigid rules to be consulted and followed to the letter.

of the binding force of the law: "Behold, the blood of the covenant which Yahweh has made with you upon the basis of all these words" (24:8, auth. trans.). In the account in Exodus 34, the covenant is also said to be put into effect by the giving of law (34:27) and the last event is the proclamation of this law to the people (34:32).[17]

The initial negotiations between Yahweh and Israel described in Exod. 19:3b–8 articulate the conceptual scheme of the covenant as fully as any in the text.[18] In vv. 4–6, Yahweh presents his qualifications (v. 4) and offers Israel a unique, exclusive relationship to the Lord of the world (v. 5b). The imagery employed to describe Israel's status combines royal and religious categories: "You shall be to me a kingdom of priests and a holy nation" (v. 6a). Israel will be a nation with a divine sovereign, thus a "kingdom of God." To be sure, Yahweh does not call himself king, but that status is implied by the designation of the people as a political entity with religious attributes. To be a sovereign means to have the power to command, to be subjects means to have the duty to obey.[19] Verse 5a makes willingness to obey Yahweh the condition of the relationship, and v. 8 has the people pledge to do so. We can say that the acceptance of Yahweh's authority by the people puts in force the relationship in which Yahweh has authority to command and Israelites are duty-bound to obey him.[20]

SUMMATION

At the outset of this chapter, the opinion of James Barr was cited to the effect that verbal communication provides a framework of meaning for God's deeds. Our study of God's speaking has carried this position forward by showing speech to be a type of divine intervention that accomplishes something in its own right. The depiction of auditions, often as a part of theophanies, evoked Yahweh's active

17. This account shifts the emphasis away from the ratification to the person of Moses. Rather strikingly, Exod. 24:9–11 seems to depict a ratification ceremony which makes no explicit reference to the law.

18. Besides Exod. 19:3b–8, I find such declarations in 20:2; 24:10; 33:12–16, 19; 34:6–7, 9, 10.

19. This is simply a textbook definition: D. Lloyd, *The Idea of Law* (Baltimore, Md.: Penguin, 1964), pp. 26ff., 170ff.

20. I use the gentilic plural "Israel*ites*" to indicate the responsibility of individuals to obey the law accepted by the community collectively.

presence in the course of human affairs. Events are inaugurated and decided by God's speaking to participants and through mediators to third parties.

God's speaking not only communicates information that explains his intervention; it also has illocutionary force. A significant portion of his utterances are performatives, utterances which create the state of affairs they describe. In the call of Moses, Yahweh issues a promise that commits him to a course of action and commands Moses and the people in slavery to act accordingly. The *trans*action at Sinai is organized around an illocutionary act which involves promises of both parties to a relationship of divine sovereignty over Israel.

To this summary I might add the observation that it is through God's illocutionary utterance that the past has continuing significance and relevance. Events succeed one another in time and the effect of any one on subsequent events diminishes as time goes on. However, God's acts have illocutionary force, a promissory character that endures through time. They remain promissory to those who recognize the biblical God today. Moreover, those who receive the promise come under the obligation to obey him. The illocutionary act of making and later owning the Sinai covenant constitutes a paradigm of the illocutionary force of past events in which God acted.

CHAPTER 7

Unity of
Action

In the last two chapters, we have been focusing our attention on the many and various ways the biblical God intervenes in the course of human affairs. The variety and multiplicity of these interventions impart the impression that God's action is irregular and episodic. The fact is that the biblical rendering of God is built up out of particular interventions. The narrators had to convince their audience of each particular act of Yahweh within a specific action. To understand this aspect of the art, we had to suspend the question of unity.

Now it is time to lift the suspension and ask pointedly: In what sense are the many and various divine acts one? If the biblical God is one, we would at least expect him to act consistently. The question is whether the unity of divine action consists only of consistency of characterization, or whether there is a unity of divine action in its own right.

It would be possible to conceive of the actions of God as episodic. His interventions might be considered a study in crisis intervention. Each would serve, on this account, to reestablish a "steady-state" universe. Each account would exemplify (if it were artistically successful) a unity of action, but the accounts taken together would simply manifest one and the same divine persona. Chronological sequence would merely be the external framework for the occasions on which humans encountered God, not the structure of a cumulative development.

I hope to show, however, that there is a much more substantial unity to God's action. Each intervention is real in its own right, yet is a step, I believe, toward the attainment of a larger purpose. Each intervention presupposes and builds upon what went before and prepares for what will follow. The goal toward which all interventions are directed is sufficiently comprehensive and profound to be the telos of the entire sequence. If these theses can be established, the biblical depiction of God's action is a unity in its own right as well as consistent with the one God.

I also hope to show that the action in which God participates (see chapter 4) finds its unity in the one action of God. Human interaction is not just punctuated by divine interventions, but is caught up in the progressive movement of God's action. No resolution is sufficiently complete to bring the story to a close; each contains in it the seeds of new crises and conflicts. This continuing tension drives the whole story forward. Since the enduring tension involves the one enduring character, the whole story drives toward a comprehensive resolution of the conflict between him and the created order.

The argument will be constructed on the evidence of large-scale ordering and of synthetic condensation. It will not be possible to concentrate on one or several texts. Rather, we will be surveying the ordering of large blocks of material and correlating them with condensations.

THE SEQUENTIAL, CUMULATIVE STRUCTURE OF BIBLICAL NARRATIVE

Narrative by its very nature is sequential and chronologically framed; that the biblical narrative should possess these traits is not surprising. What is noteworthy about the Old Testament narrative is the drive toward a single, all-embracing story line and chronological framework. To quote James Barr: "The story is, broadly speaking, a unitary story, as distinct from separate anecdotes about people who might have lived at any time: the individual units are slotted into a total framework and have their function within the literary effect of the whole."[1] It is this unitary quality of the biblical story that makes an episodic conception of God's action implausible and prompts us to seek out a more substantial unity.

---

1. "Story and History in Biblical Theology," *JR* 56/1 (1976):6.

If we were to identify the basic story line of the biblical story with a given block of Old Testament literature, it would have to be the "primary history"[2] running from creation to the exile. Narrative works that are not a part of this comprehensive story, namely, Ruth, Esther, and Jonah, can be related to it by means of chronological synchronization. Most prophetic books are dated and thus can also be synchronized. In the chronicler's work we have something of a competing account of a portion of the primary history. Among narrative works, only Job stands completely outside the story line and chronology of Genesis–2 Kings.

The primary history is made up of a host of individual narrative units. They are knit together to form one story by a number of devices. Chronology and genealogy provide a formal principle of ordering and sometimes bear the primary weight of connecting events in sequence.[3] The sequence of stories is based on the principle that the resolution of one story creates the conditions for the following one. Some sequences are tight, while others are looser, but all satisfy the basic logic of sequence. Finally, the stories work cumulatively. Each presupposes all that has happened earlier and is presupposed by all that happens subsequently. The result of such devices is a comprehensive story in which each unit is a scene or act.

The prophetic literature is not integrated into the primary history to the same degree or in the same way as the constituent stories. Rather, the prophets address the same situations as the primary history and presuppose the structure and content of the earlier portion of that story. The primary history itself is deepened and extended by the prophetic literature that is synchronized with its later portions. By a dialectical process, the prophetic books are conditioned by and contribute to the comprehensive story running through the Old Testament.

The nonnarrative books like the Psalms, Proverbs and Ecclesiastes

2. Term adopted from D. N. Freedman's class by that name at the Graduate Theological Union, Berkeley, Calif., 1965.
3. For example, the Book of Judges is little more than a string of self-contained stories sequentialized by a vague chronology.

might be said to be contemporary to the whole story.[4] Of course, the materials preserved in them can be traced with greater or lesser certainty to specific periods in Israel's history. They aspire to a kind of timelessness, however, that would make them fitting sentiments for persons located all along the story line.

THE RENDERING OF YAHWEH

The depiction of Yahweh as a character in the story corresponds to the sequential, cumulative structuring of the primary history. The earlier portions of the story introduce him, establish his identity in the mind of the reader, identify what he has said and done, and arouse expectations regarding his future manifestations. Each subsequent rendering depends upon what went before and seeks to maintain consistency of character.

The sequential, cumulative structure of the rendering of God does not mean that the reader must await the end to discern his full identity. Art requires that he be presented as a complete, fully developed character in each story. This completeness, though, involves a gathering up of the depictions that precede a given story and an open-ended quality that allows subsequent segments of the story to continue and qualify it. Consequently, the reader's synthesis of the many depictions into a single dramatic portrait is always emerging, never finished and settled.

If the identity of the biblical God assumes his past and anticipates his future action, the action itself must be sequential and cumulative. Each act of God must be a part of the progress of his overall purpose.[5] We say of a human that you achieve integrity by devoting your life to a worthy and truly comprehensive goal. When one does, every stage on life's way is full and lays the foundation for the next. The divine persona achieves unity in an analogous way. Every action

---

4. Job, too, belongs here according to my view of the matter. I take it to be a dramatized lament with the legend about the ancient, non-Israelite righteous man functioning as an artistic vehicle. Psalms and Proverbs have been associated with moments of history, too, but with even less substantial connection.

5. This does not necessarily mean that each act is a step in the unfolding of a predetermined plan. A given act might be a holding action, a regrouping, a temporary diversion, etc.

enacts his identity and fits into the sequential, cumulative movement toward a comprehensive purpose.

COMPREHENSIVE ACTION

Barr spoke of the biblical narrative as a "unitary story." This expression suggests something more than cumulative sequence. According to Aristotle, such unity lies in the oneness of the action: "The truth is that . . . in poetry the story, as an imitation of action, must represent one action, a complete whole, with its several incidents so closely connected that the transposal or withdrawal of any one of them will disjoin and dislocate the whole."[6] It is doubtful that the larger scriptural narrative could meet Aristotle's stringent demands on the interconnection of incidents, for the process by which the extant story has been shaped has left it untidy. In addition, the aesthetics of the biblical tradition are much more realistic and historylike than classical Greek epic and drama. Nonetheless, the necessity of representing one action to achieve narrative unity would apply to biblical literature as well as Greek. That means that if the biblical narrative is a unitary story, the various actions and events must exemplify the same underlying tension and contribute to its resolution.

In the following paragraphs, I will endeavor to show that the story of the primary history does represent one action. I will begin with the segment of the story that recounts the formation of the people of Israel. There are two lines of evidence that support the oneness of this action: (1) The credolike rehearsals that condense this massive story to a very brief compass; and (2), the promises which look to the conclusion of the whole story and thereby include all intervening events as stations on the way.

1. The rehearsals of God's deeds for Israel have been the center of theological discussion since G. von Rad published his study entitled "The Form-Critical Problem of the Hexateuch."[7] The text that anchored his study was Deut. 26:5–9:

---

6. *The Rhetoric and the Poetic* (New York: Modern Library, 1954), p. 234.
7. Translated in *The Problem of the Hexateuch and Other Essays* (Edinburgh and London: Oliver & Boyd, 1966), pp. 1–78.

A wandering Aramean was my father; and he went down into Egypt and sojourned there, few in number; and there he became a nation, great, mighty, and populous. And the Egyptians treated us harshly, and afflicted us, and laid upon us hard bondage. Then we cried to the Lord the God of our fathers, and the Lord heard our voice, and saw our affliction, our toil, and our oppression; and the Lord brought us out of Egypt with a mighty hand and an outstretched arm, with great terror, with signs and wonders; and he brought us into this place and gave us this land, a land flowing with milk and honey.

With great brevity and yet with poetic flourishes and dramatic tension, this liturgical confession condenses the long and complex narrative of the Hexateuch to a simple story line and unified action (from homeless wanderer to possessor of a homeland). It is decisive evidence that ancient Israel grasped the story of its formation as a unified whole.

2. The promises to the patriarchs initiate the national history and incorporate the sequences of stories running from Genesis 12 through Joshua 24 into one action.[8] Abraham and his descendants will become countless in number, will inherit the land of Canaan, and will be protected from their enemies by God. The story that follows moves tortuously but steadily toward fulfillment of these promises. In the patriarchal era, the family continues through trials and delays. The land is lived in, but not controlled. The migration to Egypt and enslavement seems to divert the momentum toward fulfillment, but actually contributes to it. The family multiplies into a large group and begins to form a people. Deliverance from slavery has the conquest of Canaan as its object. The covenant made at Sinai establishes the national constitution and institutions, and thereby prepares the people for life as a nation upon its land. The movement is delayed again by the rebellions in the wilderness, but finally comes to fruition under Joshua.

8. The story of creation, fall and primordial history set the stage for the national history by dramatizing the fundamental conflict between the Creator and his human creatures; the call of Abraham, which promises him that he will be a blessing to the nations, is the beginning of the resolution of the conflict. See G. von Rad, *Genesis* (Philadelphia: Westminster Press, 1961), pp. 148–150, 154–56.

When Joshua calls an assembly of the people to renew their allegiance to Yahweh (Joshua 24), the promises made to Abraham have been fulfilled. The tensions and challenges that arose in the course of the movement from promise to fulfillment, which in fact constitute the critical turning points of the story (namely, the events of the Mosaic period), are also resolved. Now life on the land itself will produce the issues to be resolved, as Joshua ominously warns them.

Although the action comes to fulfillment in Joshua 24, the second segment of the story (Judges–2 Kings) does not have a separate, independent action. Rather, it is essentially the reversal of the action just completed. The prophets bring this paradoxical unity to dramatic expression in their condensations of Israel's history with Yahweh, e.g., Hos. 11:1–2a:

> When Israel was a child, I loved him,
>   and out of Egypt I called my son.
> The more I called them,
>   the more they went from me.

These two short couplets encompass the essential history of Israel up to Yahweh's intervention to resolve the contradiction. It demonstrates clearly that the entire primary history can be grasped as a single action.

It would be possible for us to identify the promises and warnings that project the course of action running through the second segment of the primary history, but that seems unnecessary. I think that the case has been made that Israel's unitary story has a single action. We need only add that Yahweh's role in the action is decisive. He is the one who promises and intervenes at the strategic points to bring the formative history to its completion. It is against him that the people of Israel rebel in the second segment and his act of judgment resolves the contradiction, or perhaps we should say brings this phase to its denouement.

ESCHATOLOGY

When and to what literature the term "eschatology" should be applied is the subject of unending debate among biblical scholars and theologians. Following von Rad, Wolff and Hanson,[9] I will categorize classical prophecy and early apocalyptic as eschatological. By that I mean that this literature announces a divine intervention which will resolve the conflict between God and his human creatures once for all. That this description fits classical prophecy and early apocalyptic will be argued in the course of the following paragraphs. However, the place to begin is with the conclusion of the primary history.

According to the sequential logic of the primary history, the story would never end. Each story leads to another. Each resolution of tension between God's will and the human situation creates a new tension. The work does, however, stop with the exile. Is this an historical accident, that is, did the author write the story up to his own time and no new author take up the task of continuing it? If this explanation were adopted, the primary story line does not so much end as break off. One could, consequently, take the chronicler's continuation of the story into the postexilic period as a legitimate addition to the primary story.

The alternative to interpreting the cessation of the primary history as an accident is to see it as a theological necessity. The large-scale actions that tie the independent stories and historical periods together reach to the exile but no further. If the author has appropriated the prophetic message, the exile is not simply one event in a series, but a final event rendering the continuation of God's history with his people impossible. The story of the struggle between God and his people cannot go on as before, for the divine judgment resolves that story.

The primary history does hint at a continuation of the story. The last event reported is not the exile, but Jehoiachin's release from prison and elevation to the Babylonian court (2 Kings 25:27–30). This event seems to foreshadow a reestablishment of the monarchy.[10]

9. G. von Rad, *Old Testament Theology,* vol. 2 (Edinburgh and London: Oliver & Boyd, 1965), pp. 112–19; P. Hanson, *The Dawn of Apocalyptic* (Philadelphia: Fortress Press, 1975), pp. 10ff.; cp. H.W. Wolff, "The Understanding of History in the Old Testament Prophets," in *Essays on Old Testament Hermeneutics,* C. Westermann, ed. (Richmond, Va.: John Knox Press, 1963), pp. 336ff.

10. Cf. G. von Rad, *Studies in Deuteronomy* (London: SCM Press, 1953), p. 90.

Of greater import is the homily addressed to the Judean exiles in Deut. 30:1–3:

> And when all these things come upon you . . . and you call them to mind among all the nations where the Lord your God has driven you, and return to the Lord your God . . . and obey his voice in all that I command you this day, with all your heart and with all your soul, then the Lord your God will restore your fortunes, and have compassion upon you, and he will gather you again from all the peoples where the Lord your God has scattered you.

This passage can be interpreted to promise a continuation of the history of Yahweh and his people on approximately the same terms as before the exile. However, it can be interpreted eschatologically: a decisive divine intervention will break the logic of that history and initiate something radically new. The prophetic sounding promise in v. 6 supports this eschatological interpretation: "And the Lord your God will circumcise your heart and the heart of your offspring, so that you will love the Lord your God with all your heart and with all your soul, that you may live." The exile will be ended not by a restoration of conditions as before, but by an unconditional salvation.

If the promises made to the exiles by the deuteronomistic historian are eschatological, the exile itself has that significance. It is indeed the conclusion of the story beginning with creation. The exile both resolves the story and creates an ultimate tension needing resolution. It resolves the story by bringing the conflict between Yahweh and Israel to an end. It creates an "ultimate" tension by promising that the rebellious heart of the people which caused the divine judgment will be replaced by an obedient, loyal heart. To do that would be to bring the tension between God's will and the whole of human history to an end.

The interpretation of the exile just given derives from and depends upon the classical prophets. It was these spokesmen for Yahweh, running from Amos and Hosea through Isaiah and Micah to Jeremiah and Ezekiel, who announced beforehand that the exile was coming and that it would be a decisive and final divine intervention. It was also this line which held out the hope that a new, obedient Israel would be born in the ashes of judgment. The deuteronomistic homily to the exiles is really an echo of this thundering voice from on high.

The fulcrum of the preexilic prophetic message was the announcement of judgment. It was Israel's guilt and irreversible history of corruption that necessitated Yahweh's decisive intervention. But precisely as a fulcrum, the act of judgment opened up the possibility of a new beginning. Beginning with Hosea and continuing through his successors, this possibility is the subject of promise.

The logic of the prophetic announcement of salvation is that the struggle between God and his creatures cannot go on endlessly without resolution. Since it was God's action in Israel's history that was to overcome this conflict, ending it in annihilating judgment would mean God's admission of failure.[11] The promises which initiated and animated Israel's history must therefore still be valid despite judgment.[12] The bond between Yahweh and his people is once for all and therefore encompasses the dark hours of enmity and punishment in the day of salvation.

The inner tension within the course of history leading to judgment was Israel's wayward heart, so the fundamental resolution of this history will be a transformation of the heart (Hos. 2:16–22; 14:1–7; Isa. 1:21–31; Jer. 31:31–34). The final battleground is the human heart, and in particular, the heart of God's own people, and victory here is eschatological indeed.[13]

Among the preexilic prophets, only Isaiah extends the coming divine intervention to include the nations of the world in Yahweh's saving work.[14] He articulates hopes for a new world order arising out of the destruction of the Assyrian empire by Yahweh:

> I will break the Assyrian in my land,
>   and upon my mountains trample him under foot;
> and his yoke shall depart from them,
>   and his burden from their shoulder.
> This is the purpose that is purposed
>   concerning the whole earth;

11. This is not actually said in the prophetic canon until Ezekiel, namely, the motive of "vindicating the holiness" of his name for saving Israel (Ezek. 36:20–32).

12. I would take that as the implication of the passages that repeat or echo old promises in the new: Hosea 2; Isa. 2:1ff.; 11:1ff.; Jer. 31:1ff., 20, etc.

13. If the scourges of finite existence were divine judgment, it follows that they too would be eliminated by the change of the heart.

14. I take Micah 4—5 to be secondary, save for 5:1ff.

and this is the hand that is stretched out
  over all the nations.

(Isa. 14:25–26)

When Yahweh acts to deliver Israel from its oppressor, it will have universal effect and open the way for a reign of peace.[15]

The anonymous prophet known as Second Isaiah has a similar hope associated with Israel's deliverance from Babylonian exile by Cyrus. At one point the peoples of the world are told:

Turn to me and be saved,
all the ends of the earth!
  For I am God, and there is no other.
By myself I have sworn . . .:
To me every knee shall bow,
every tongue shall swear.

(45:22–23)

The resolution of Israel's history is the resolution of all human history.

Given the eschatological interpretation imposed upon the exile by the prophets, it would be theologically impossible for the primary history to continue on, tracing the course of postexilic history as it does the preexilic period. The only event that could have theological import after the exile is the ending of it in the coming of salvation for Israel and the world. The restoration of Jerusalem and reinstatement of cultic life does not move the story of God's struggle with his creatures any nearer resolution.[16]

The beginnings of apocalyptic literature can be traced to the exile and the early restoration period.[17] The followers of Second Isaiah and Ezekiel initially shared the hope of an eschatological intervention of Yahweh. However, those who traced their lineage to Ezekiel gained power in Jerusalem and throughout Judaism, settling for an eschatological veneer legitimizing power politics, while the disciples of Second Isaiah continued to wait for a saving event worthy of the name. In the course of their waiting and hopeless struggle with the

---

15. Cf. N. Gottwald, *All the Kingdoms of the Earth* (New York: Harper & Row, 1964), pp. 183–84, 196–203.
16. Ezra and Nehemiah may be seeking to assert the contrary, but it is striking that God's action has essentially disappeared from the story.
17. Following P. Hanson, *The Dawn of Apocalyptic.*

priestly establishment, the group responsible for Third Isaiah moved progressively toward a form of expression characteristic of later apocalyptic literature: "The essential characteristics of apocalyptic eschatology are drawn together into a coherent whole in Isaiah 65: the present era is evil; a great judgment separating the good from the evil and the world to come is imminent; a newly created world of peace and blessing ordained for the faithful lies beyond that judgment."[18]

To my mind, apocalyptic eschatology was the logical and legitimate extension of prophetic eschatology.[19] In apocalyptic the final intervention of God takes more and more the shape of the absolute transformation of creation and human existence that is implicit in the concept. Because the authors of apocalyptic chose to remain anonymous and append their utterances to prophetic books, they literally extend prophetic eschatology.[20] They round off the unitary action of God in the story of the Old Testament.

THE IDEA OF THE "PLAN OF GOD"

The thesis argued in this chapter resembles the idea of a divine plan of salvation sufficiently to deserve a brief discussion. The idea that the Bible contains a "plan of salvation" has been a staple of Reformed and Free Church theology and piety. In biblical theology the idea was restated in terms of a "saving history" by such men as J. T. Beck and J. Chr. K. von Hofmann in the nineteenth century and brought into the middle of the twentieth by Oscar Cullmann.[21] According to this conceptual scheme, the Old and New Testaments exhibit a divine plan or economy of salvation that can be traced phase by phase.

The concept of salvation history is substantiated by our findings.

18. Ibid., 160.
19. This is not the opinion of von Rad, *Old Testament Theology*, vol. 2, pp. 301ff. Even Hanson, ibid., pp. 402ff., seems to lack enthusiasm for apocalyptic eschatology.
20. Compare the position taken by Brevard Childs with respect to the prophetic books: "The Canonical Shape of the Prophetic Literature," *Interpretation* 32/1 (1978):46–55.
21. On Beck and von Hofmann, cp. von Rad, *Old Testament Theology*, vol. 2, p. 362; Cullmann's *Christ and Time: The Primitive Christian Conception of Time and History* is available in a translation by F. V. Filson (Philadelphia: Westminster Press, 1950).

The biblical story is sequential and cumulative and exhibits a single action under the purposive guidance of Yahweh. It may seem ironical that our argument confirmed a position considered conservative within the theological community, but theological fashion should not close our minds.

The concept of saving history, however, has two crucial shortcomings. First, it contradicts the open texture of each historical moment. The biblical rendering of Yahweh does not, save perhaps in Daniel, present him as having foreordained every twist and turn of history or as having known at every juncture what he will do. There is even reason to speak of God's failure when Israel must be judged for its disobedience—not an irreversible failure, but a situation that thwarted his stated intentions and expectations, and required a new course of action.

Second, the concept of a saving history unfolding according to a logical plan distances the reader from the narrative present. This distancing is caused by the procedure of fitting each narrative or utterance into the overall plan.[22] Thus, the theory works against the objective of the biblical rendering of God, namely, evoking his presence and delineating his identity.

In view of these defects in the concept of saving history as it has been worked out by biblical theologians, it is better to avoid the language of "plan" or "history of salvation" in favor of that of a sequential, cumulative action of God which runs through Scripture and presses toward final resolution.

22. All theological reflection has this danger, but the *Heilsgeschichte* scheme is particularly corrupting. One is encouraged to believe in a plan of salvation more than in the persona who acts.

PART THREE

THE RENDERING OF
YAHWEH AND THE
IDENTITY OF GOD

CHAPTER 8

The Reality of the Biblical God

Biblical literature presses the claim to reality with especial urgency. It refuses to fall quietly into the category of mere imaginative literature. It refuses to fit our definitions of myth, epic, poetry, fiction or historiography. It refuses to entertain us, inform us, or purge our emotions. Rather, it seeks to define us and lead us into the way of truth. To cite one noted literary critic, Erich Auerbach, the "Bible's claim to truth is not only more urgent than Homer's, it is tyrannical—it excludes all other claims."[1] The biblical God insists on being the only God, and the world created by this God is presented as the only true world. Nothing in life can exist independent of the biblical story and everything has its proper place within it. The narrative seeks to "subject us, and if we refuse to be subjected we are rebels."[2]

Auerbach's innuendo that the biblical God is a tyrant is rhetorical exaggeration, for a tyrant is a ruler who imposes his will without legitimate authority; Yahweh bases his claims upon his legitimacy. Indeed, it is precisely the capacity of the biblical rendering of God to convince us of Yahweh's legitimacy that makes it so effective. Marduk and Zeus are tyrants, but not Yahweh. Prometheus has a righteous cause against Zeus, but Jeremiah and Job appeal to the justice of God against his actions.

Our task in this chapter is to exhibit the features of the biblical rendering of Yahweh that press his claims to reality upon us and elicit our confession that he is God indeed. It will be organized along

---

1. *Mimesis* (Garden City, N.Y.: Anchor/Doubleday & Co., 1953), p. 12.
2. Ibid.

the lines of the three classical types of argument for the existence of God: the ontological, the cosmological, and the moral-existential. There are obvious differences between dramatic depiction and discursive reasoning, but they are more closely related than one might think. The formal logical formulation of reasons for believing in God abstracts from the depiction of the biblical God. We can, therefore, invert the process by exhibiting how the rendering of God elicits conviction.[3]

The capacity of the biblical rendering of God to evoke his presence and establish the identity of the one present corresponds to Anselm's ontological argument.[4] The capacity of the biblical persona to claim a role in the dramas of human history corresponds to the cosmological arguments. The capacity of the biblical depiction to arouse religious dread and reverence in the audience corresponds to the moral-existential confirmation of God's existence.

These three confirmations of the reality of the biblical God work in tandem. The characterization of Yahweh evoking his presence and delineating his identity has logical priority. It is this persona who compels recognition in the dramas of history and prompts our existential response. If we could not find him in history, however, or did not meet him in subjective experience, we would not be able to entertain him as a dramatis persona.

Objections can be raised to these arguments. It is possible to entertain Yahweh as an imaginary being, but to resist the claim he makes to be the one true God. There are personal experiences, social perceptions and intellectual convictions that transform the encounter into an occasion for offense rather than conviction. It is not our purpose, however, to address objections, but rather to present the claims.

---

3. I have J. Moltmann, *Theology of Hope* (New York and Evanston: Harper & Row, 1967), pp. 50–84, to credit for exhibiting the argument basis of theological positions and suggesting the triadic structure of the arguments.

4. *Monologion.* Anselm's formulation of his argument as a prayer is an indispensable component of the argument: one confirms through reflection on his identity the indubitable reality of the deity present in the dialogue of prayer. This corresponds to the biblical depiction of Yahweh, which establishes a dialogical relationship between God and the audience and confirms the reality of this "thou" in the delineation of his identity.

THE CAPACITY OF THE CHARACTERIZATION TO CONVINCE

What prompts an audience to entertain the reality of the characters presented to it? There must be criteria of authenticity that are met by successful characterization which makes fictional, and nonfictional, personages ring true to reality. I would suggest that it is their stage presence, the coherence of their identity, and their ability to illumine who we are. If the biblical God is capable of arousing our conviction, the biblical rendering of this persona must likewise satisfy these components of dramatic truth. Let us reflect upon each of these in turn.

By "stage presence," I mean the representation of character in such a way that the persona is not only delineated, but actually evoked. The author must represent a thinking, feeling, acting persona who confronts the audience as a "presence." The audience must be made to relate to the persona not as he or she, but as "you." By a magical act of make-believe, a genuine personal relationship can be struck across the ontological gap between an imaginary person and the one imagining.

Yahweh confronts us in biblical literature as a dramatis persona with presence. He is not an abstract entity or cardboard figure, but a genuine "thou" with passion, vitality, mystery, subtlety and force. We the audience can enter into him imaginatively to experience what he experiences and into the scene to sense his presence as the other personae do.

Prayer and praise are intrinsic ingredients of biblical literature. They are interspersed throughout the narratives and prophecies as well as collected together in the Psalms. What further proof is needed that the rendering of Yahweh draws forth an I-thou relationship with his audience? By means of this address language, the audience suddenly finds itself in the drama.

By "coherent identity," I mean the delineation of a character with specific features, compatible with one another, and indivisibly synthesized in an "I." We might say, metaphorically, that an author sets out a series of game rules for each character, rules by which a character plays himself or herself. The audience must grasp the rules of the game to enter imaginatively into the character and to satisfy the intellect's thirst for understanding. Consistency of characterization is a necessary component of coherence, for identity consists not only of individuality but also continuity in time.

Yahweh's identity is established and maintained in the course of the biblical story. The authors of Scripture identify him as having specific personal traits, a personal history, and a definable nature. Because he is God, he is capable of paradoxical antitheses and shattering new departures while remaining consistent with himself. We the readers learn to grasp the rules of biblical God-language both by intuition and reflection and thereby participate in the process of imagining him into character.

Yahweh's identity confirms the reality of his presence. A God who existed only in our imagination could not be entertained in our imagination. Unlike a human character who is finite (located in a particular time and place), this deity by nature cannot be limited to the literary rendering of him. Hamlet is exhausted in the dramatic rendering, Moses in the depiction and its historical rootage, but Yahweh must be inexhaustible to be the character that he is. For this God to be present in a given moment in time at a given place and to participate in a given action, he must be present in every time and place and participate in every action.[5] When we encounter him as present in the literature, we are encountering one who exists in reality.

One cannot take a fictional character with the seriousness that Yahweh requires of everyone who entertains him as a possibility. One can always say of an imaginary character that it makes no difference whether he or she is historical for the appreciation of his or her truth. Yahweh, by contrast, insists on being taken as exclusively real: "You shall have no other god before (besides) me" (Exod. 20:3). To engage this dramatis persona in his dramatic reality, one must recognize his claim to be God alone and God indeed.

Finally, this God exercises his sovereignty over author and audience. When an author ventured a rendering of God, he or she sur-

---

5. Note the way Amos can generalize from Israel's history to Yahweh's lordship over all: "Did I not bring up Israel from the land of Egypt, and the Philistines from Caphtor and the Syrians from Kir?" (9:7).

rendered authorial prerogative to establish perspective on the action to the one portrayed. The quest for dramatic truth and moral right was embodied in the rendering of Yahweh's perspective and purpose. The reader, too, must accept the perspective established by Yahweh's presence and action. This God is righteous in all that he does and none of his purposes can be thwarted (Job 42:2). The only way the reader can evade God's sovereignty is to refuse to entertain him as a dramatis persona.

Finally, characters must establish a certain conaturality with the audience. Through cultural tradition, observation and introspection, we develop a sense of what it means to be human, how humans think and feel, what heights and depths are possible for us, and so forth. A character must conform to our image of the human and/or convince us to extend it. If the purpose of drama, narrative and the other histrionic arts is to "hold a mirror up to nature" (Hamlet to the players), the establishment of conaturality is a necessary and vital component of artistic communication.

It hardly needs to be argued that Yahweh establishes a significant degree of conaturality with the audience, for anthropomorphisms have been a source of embarrassment to believers and of ridicule by cultured despisers. What the depiction does is fit and extend our image of a thinking, feeling, acting dramatis persona who possesses the qualifications of a deity. By an act of make-believe, we can imagine his unique perception and response to the human drama.

It might be objected that Yahweh's conaturality with humans actually counts against his reality. Someone might argue, say, that this God is an alienated self-projection, a being with the capacities of a human being but not the defects.[6] It would be ironic if this were so, for the biblical rendering of God provides the original critique of idolatry. Did the biblical authors fall victim to the very thing they condemned? To answer in the affirmative, it must be shown that the deity could under no conditions exhibit the presence, identity and comprehensibility necessary for effective characterization. Within its own dramatic terms, the biblical rendering of Yahweh preserves the

6. Cf. L. Feuerbach, *The Essence of Christianity* (New York: Harper & Row, 1958).

infinite qualitative distinction between God and every human persona. Only if it is contradictory in principle for deity to be a dramatis persona can one say that Yahweh is a human writ large.

What is at stake in this argument is whether human beings can legitimately grasp their relation to ultimate reality via the dramatic mode. Once it is stated in that way, one can see how arbitrary a negative is. The best reply is to show that we encounter ultimate reality in the biblical God. This encounter takes place in the dramatic context of our lives and evokes in us the sense of the holy.

CONFIRMING THE REALITY OF GOD
IN THE EXPERIENCE OF THE WORLD

The aim of this section is to confirm the reality of the God rendered in Scripture by exhibiting his presence in history and nature. The argument corresponds to the cosmological arguments for the existence of God, but proceeds from the identity and recognition of God to the finitude of the world, rather than the reverse. The thrust of the argument is that the rendering of God convinces us of his reality by rendering the world in which he acts as true to life—ambiguous, mysterious and tragic—and yet meaningful and promising.

A good place to begin is with an explanation of why the argument proceeds from God to world and not the reverse. The classical cosmological arguments begin with an analysis of the finite world and endeavor to infer the existence of a necessary being from the contradiction of a self-generating cosmos. The rendering of Yahweh in Scripture moves in the opposite direction. He is depicted as creating the world and ruling history, and from this we conclude that the world cannot be interpreted as self-generated and self-contained. The biblical order cannot be simply chalked up to the alleged mythical or prelogical mind set of Israelite religion. It is not at all certain that the human mind can infer the contingency of the cosmos without reference to the unconditioned nor is it obvious that humanity is not lord of its own destiny without reference to the one who overthrows the mighty and raises up the lowly. The biblical modus operandi has the virtue of positing God and world together in dialectical interaction.

Human affairs, rather than the finite world as a whole, are the primary focus of biblical literature. This focus was by no means obvious to the ancients. Although there was genuine interest in human affairs and history among Israel's neighbors, the great myths celebrating the exploits of gods and goddesses concern themselves with the origin and rhythm of the natural world. Clearly these peoples subordinated the drama of history to the rhythm of the cosmos. Biblical literature does the opposite, relegating the origin of the cosmos and rhythm of nature to the status of backdrop for the human drama.[7]

The biblical attention to history is attributable to the epistemological dialectic of tradition and identification. Yahweh was recognized by his capacity to establish his identity with the God already known in tradition. The tradition conditioned the moment of recognition by providing the identity of the one recognized and the act of recognition conditioned the tradition by identifying in it the one recognized. Only the God recognized in the tradition could establish his identity in the present, and only the traditions in which God was already known could facilitate the moment of recognition.

The moment of recognition was not an occasion in which timeless truth entered the human mind; rather, it was God's act of self-identification and as such entered into his identity.[8] The epistemological event of recognition was simultaneously an ontological event. The biblical God attains his identity in interaction with those who recognize him. The tradition preserved memories of the events of recognition because they belonged to the identity of the one recognized.

If we are to speak of the biblical God in human history, we must grant tradition a constitutive role in our epistemology and ontology. Tradition cannot be considered the enemy of truth, but the ingredient that makes history possible and makes understanding at least potentially possible.[9] If this is granted, it is possible to affirm that

7. I am aware that this observation echoes the now discredited biblical theology movement. I must confess that I am a child of that movement and desire to preserve its concerns and rescue as many of its concepts as possible. I hope I have avoided the ambiguities and simplifications that brought it to a halt.

8. For the basic distinction I am drawing here, cf. Søren Kierkegaard, *Philosophical Fragments* (Princeton: Princeton University Press, 1962).

9. To be sure, there is no guarantee that ancestral wisdom and passion are true, but if there is any truth accessible to our species it must be in some sense contained in tradition.

God is recognizable within the history in which he is already known. The moment of recognition was not an interpretation imposed upon the raw data of experience, but a genuine discovery of the presence of one whose identity is embedded in the collective life of Israel. Just as rights and duties are embedded in the legal and cultural tradition of a legal community and "found" by judges in cases before the bar,[10] so the biblical authors "found" the God known in their tradition in the materials they were to render.

The rendering of the biblical God is limited (with the exception of the primordial history) to the events which Israel itself experienced and in which the recognition of Yahweh was a component of the experience. Of course Israelites believed he was active elsewhere, but their own story was the one in which his activity was recognized and remembered. The uniqueness of Israel's history does not lie in the events per se, but in the fact that the recognition of Yahweh was a constituent factor in these events.

How can it be claimed that God's presence in events is truly objective if one must enter this tradition to discern him? The objectivity of Israel's experience can only be indirectly confirmed, for there are no set standards by which we can judge a tradition in its totality. If the biblical account of human affairs is realistic in general and historically founded when necessary, we can say that there is good reason to believe that an objective reality is manifested in it. To its realism and historicity we now turn.

The everyday meaning of the term "realism" is rather slippery, for we tend to count as realistic what we have been conditioned to

10. So Ronald Dworkin in *Taking Rights Seriously* (Cambridge, Mass.: Harvard University Press, 1977), whose position on this matter is beautifully summarized by a reviewer, Michael Walzer: "Taking rights seriously means attending to the text of the Constitution, to the interpretations and shared understandings of that text developed over the years, to subsequent legislation and court decisions, to institutional history, and to the principles of our common morality. Out of this mass of information, the judge must construct a political theory . . . which reflects our convictions, which describes the status of individuals in our society. And then, confronted with a hard case, the judge discovers rather than invents the rights that he enforces: his decision is a 'finding'. . . . Dworkin's fundamental claim is that rights exist, deeply embedded in the collective life of our constitutional regime." *TNR* 176/26 (June 25, 1977): 29–30.

count. However, it is possible to develop an objective definition of a style of representation and contrast it to other styles. Erich Auerbach has done just that. His definition of realism involves such features as the mixture of styles, multidimensional characterization, varying illumination, historical background, and representation as the telos (not merely illustration) of communication.[11] These stylistic features characterize a body of literature, of which the Bible is only one small portion. Hence, the characterization of biblical literature as realistic in contrast to Homeric epic is a judgment that can be verified or disputed by reference to public criteria and evidence.[12]

The realism of biblical literature supports the claim that God is acting within the world of common experience. Negatively, belief in this God does not require us to sacrifice our perception of the harsh and puzzling facts of life. On the contrary, it prompts us to recognize our fallibility and perversity and the corruption and finitude of the world in which we live. The action of God is manifest within it, so it is a significant world, but it remains a world in conflict with its own peace.

It has already been acknowledged that one important element of the Old Testament representation of reality no longer strikes the modern reader as realistic: God's miraculous interventions in nature and history. To most of us, some of these interventions seem mere coincidence while others appear altogether unbelievable. The cognitive dissonance can be overcome, however, if we recognize that aesthetic sensibility has been altered in the course of time, but can be recaptured by an imaginative act. We can easily grasp that occurrences which evoked the divine became historically significant for the participants and thereby shaped the course and outcome of events.

Many scriptural passages perform their function simply by their verisimilitude, but others require historical verification because they attest to events that are purported to redefine reality. These events have what we have called "illocutionary force," e.g., promising,

---

11. *Mimesis*, pp. 489–92; also pp, 1–20, passim.
12. I should acknowledge my debt to H. Frei's *Eclipse of Biblical Narrative* (New Haven, Conn.: Yale University Press, 1974).

commanding or declaring a verdict. If the event itself did not occur or occurred in an unrecognizable form, the promise, command or verdict is not in force.[13] The prophets, too, submitted their announcements to the judgment of history.

Of course, it is not a settled question that a fundamental dramatic continuity has been maintained between event and representation and between prophecy and fulfillment. Critical historians differ in their reconstructions, and theologians would differ on the degree and kind of continuity that would be theologically sufficient. This is not the place to assess whether biblical literature meets this test of truth, if it could ever be decided once and for all. It has been my purpose, rather, to establish the proposition that confirmation of the reality of the biblical God's action in history must include a sophisticated, careful and judicious verification of critical historical events.

The question of the historicity of the biblical narrative also arises with regard to its cumulative sequence and underlying action. Can we say that this way of interpreting Israelite history is genuinely objective, or is it a pattern imposed upon the chaos of events? From within the tradition, the cumulative action of God was certainly a *finding*. With an experience of life shaped by the identity of God enacted in events with illocutionary force, the authors encountered each new turn of the story as serving a comprehensive, universal purpose.

Again, it is beyond the purview of this essay to venture a judgment as to the objective validity of this interpretation of Israel's history, or even to say how such a judgment could be made. It is obvious, though, that the final denouement toward which this history moves has not come to pass. Indeed, the "delay of the parousia" hangs over the entire biblical drama as a great question mark. Some would take its failure to materialize as a refutation of the truth claims of the biblical faith. Nothing, however, stands in the way of taking the promise of a denouement as a promise to us as well. The drive of the biblical story toward a final resolution is itself a confirmation of this promise, and all of human history can be interpreted

13. Cf. Paul on the resurrection of Jesus: "If Christ has not been raised, your faith is futile and you are still in your sins" (1 Cor. 15:17). Events like the exodus, conquest and kingship, as well as the exile, have a similar illocutionary force that would be vitiated by historical discomfirmation.

as moving secretly and paradoxically toward this end.[14]

Finally, we have arrived at the concept with which the classical cosmological arguments begin, namely, the contingency of the world. It was suggested at the outset that the contingency of the world cannot be inferred without reference to the unconditioned. We do not realize that the order and process to which we belong has no more substance than we ourselves. Within the tradition that recognizes the Creator, we do experience the cosmic order and process as contingent, as creatures before God. However, recognition of the Creator did not arise from the experience of nature as such, but from the moments of recognition that constituted Israel's history. The recognition of the God who is present in history carried with it as a corollary the recognition of the same as Creator. Because the knowledge of the Creator was mediated through historical situations, it cannot be said that the experience of the finite world as a creature in the presence of God is an independent confirmation of his reality.

To summarize, the reality of the God rendered in Scripture is confirmed by his presence and action in history. Human affairs are the focus of the biblical depiction of God because he achieves his identity in interaction with those who recognize him in their present by means of their tradition. By means of tradition, Israelites *found* their God present in their everyday lives. Although the objectivity of their experience of history cannot be demonstrated, it can be indirectly confirmed by the realism of the biblical narrative and the potential verifiability of individual illocutionary events and the cumulative movement of the overall story. The nonoccurrence of the promised denouement may be taken as disconfirmation or as occasion for taking the promise as promise to us. Finally, the recognition of the biblical God within a particular history reveals the contingency of all reality.

THE RELIGIOUS CAPACITY OF THE BIBLICAL GOD

The capacity of biblical literature to convince us of the reality of Yahweh requires a subjective or experiential confirmation. By that,

---

14. Cf. W. Pannenberg, *Basic Questions in Theology*, vol. 1 (Philadelphia: Fortress Press, 1970), particularly pp. 15–80.

I mean that the depiction of this God must generate those states of feeling which Rudolf Otto identified as evidencing encounter with the holy.[15] If the depiction could not evoke these states of feeling, Yahweh would not satisfy the religious yearnings of the human spirit.

When the authors of biblical literature ascribed deity to Yahweh, they assumed the types of experiences by which an ancient Near Eastern deity was known. Their religious experience involved states of feeling appropriate to encounters with the supernatural: a sense of awe, uncanniness, majesty, urgency and attraction. Israel could recognize Yahweh as a deity because he possessed the power and glory of deity to a superlative degree and elicited the appropriate response from those he encountered.[16]

At the heart of the moments of recognition of Yahweh was the manifestation of holiness. Moses was prepared to recognize Yahweh by the burning bush. When he was warned to show proper reverence, he knew he was dealing with a divine reality. The exchange itself exemplifies the mood of a sacred encounter (see chapter 2). As a necessary component of the moment of recognition, the experience of holiness is a constituent of God's very identity.

The biblical rendering of God not only reports the experience of the holy, but generates it (by dramatic means) in the reader. For those of us who have grown up in a religious tradition informed by Scripture, the reading and reenactment of biblical encounters is the source of much of our religious experience. We know the awesomeness of the holy because we have entered into the encounters of Moses and Isaiah with the biblical God. Our ministers have raised up the burning wrath of this God before our eyes and then driven us into his merciful arms.

Ultimately the biblical claim to truth depends upon the capacity of the biblical God to be the one who is encountered in every experience of the holy. Yahweh is not simply one of a class of beings sharing the attributes conducive to religious experience, but rather, he is the exclusive claimant to these attributes. This means that

15. *The Idea of the Holy* (New York: Oxford University Press, 1958).
16. We might say that Yahweh's holiness *placed* him ontologically. If human characters can be placed in experience, so must a deity. There must be a realm of experience that confirms the reality of deity, or we could not entertain them in our imagination.

Yahweh cannot be a symbolic figure of a dimension of reality that transcends him and can be experienced apart from him in other symbolic figures. If Yahweh evokes the encounter with the holy, he is the identity of the holy. He is the one already known in all religious experience, requiring only an encounter at the burning bush to be recognized as the one already known.

One aspect of the holy that is indelibly stamped on the biblical mind is moral perfection. The Holy One of Israel is set off from his creatures not only by his infinite power, wisdom and majesty, but also by his righteousness and justice. The creature who encountered him was in danger of being consumed by the righteous wrath of the one before whom human righteousness is "filthy rags." To quote Isaiah, "Woe is me! For I am lost; for I am a man of unclean lips, and I dwell in the midst of a people of unclean lips" (Isa. 6:5).

The moral connotation of divine holiness is also exhibited in the language of the Holiness Code, in which the commands and judgments imposed upon Israel are grounded in the motive: "You shall be holy, for I the Lord your God am holy" (Lev. 19:1). The people must attain holiness by seeking to conform to the holy—righteous and just—will of God. The sense of moral obligation is thus built into the experience of the holiness of God. Likewise, the feeling of guilt for moral and spiritual failure is grounded in the encounter with the holy God. The yearning for wholeness and integrity is answered by divine forgiveness made available through sacrificial ritual.

The rendering of the biblical God presupposes the common human experience of the sense of sacred obligation, guilt and yearning for wholeness. These are embedded in the human experience of the holy and come to expression again and again in myth and ritual. It is not a case of "positing" a religious foundation of moral experience (Kant), for the link is built into the experience of the holy. Yahweh is recognizable as a deity because he is able to evoke these primal human experiences. He establishes his exclusive claim to holiness by the unique force with which he does so.

To summarize, the rendering of Yahweh is also confirmed by his capacity to evoke a sense of the holy in humans. He possesses this capacity as a deity. By claiming to be the one and only God, he claims to be the sole source of religious experience. A prime component of his holiness is his moral perfection. Encounter with him engenders a sense of sacred obligation, guilt and yearning for wholeness. Here again he confirms the reality of his deity.

SUMMATION

It has been our objective in this chapter to account for and justify the capacity of biblical literature to convince us of the reality of the biblical God. We organized our reflection along the lines of the three classical arguments for the existence of God.

The capacity of the biblical rendering of God to evoke his presence and delineate his identity corresponds, I suggested, to the ontological argument. We are drawn into a relation with Yahweh via the imagination, but then we realize that he must actually exist to be entertained in the imagination.

But there is an objection to depicting the deity as a dramatis persona: it involves anthropomorphic conceptions. This objection would deny, in effect, the capacity of ultimate reality to interact with finite beings. The way to establish that it can so interact is to substantiate that he has.

The capacity of the biblical depiction of God to be recognized in the course of human events corresponds to the cosmological argument. The biblical narrative focuses on the events in which Yahweh's action was recognized by the human participants. He could be recognized because the tradition which identified him was a constituent part of that history. The event of recognition itself entered into tradition as a component of Yahweh's identity. It is not possible simply to demonstrate the objectivity of Israel's experience of history, but it can be confirmed by its realism. The capacity of the narrative to convince us that the events narrated and persons portrayed are true to life confirms that Yahweh establishes his reality in the very world which we confront. In addition to this general realism, there are events which have illocutionary force and for that reason must be confirmed by critical history to bear their weight. The cumulative action of the biblical story seems to elude confirmation, for it depends upon the promise of a denouement being fulfilled. To confirm it, we must receive the promise as promise to us. If we do, all finite reality becomes contingent before the Creator.

Finally, the capacity of the biblical rendering of God to evoke the states of feeling appropriate to the experience of the holy corresponds to the moral-existential argument. The religious quality of the encounter confirms that Yahweh is a deity. If he is a deity, he is the one who is encountered in every experience of the holy. The sense of sacred obligation, guilt and yearning for wholeness derives from encounter with the Holy One, confirming that the God who enacts his identity in the story leading to a resolution of the conflict between him and his creatures is God indeed.

CHAPTER 9

Divine Initiative in
Human Imagination

If the biblical rendering of Yahweh has the capacity to convince us of his reality, he himself must be its author. We humans are quite capable of bestowing existence upon the creatures of our imagination, but it would be illusory to seek the living God in ourselves. The imaginative process by which we give dramatic life to the biblical God can be nothing more than a vehicle of his self-identification. Without imagination we could not know or encounter him, but God's identification with our characterization is required to give it reality and truth.

Each of the three arguments presented in chapter 8 for the reality of the biblical God implies that he is the author of his own identity and presence. First, the power and authority to evoke God's presence and delineate his identity cannot ultimately belong to his creatures, but must be granted from on high. Second, the rendering of God cannot be imposed upon the raw data of experience, but must be found in the events of history in which he is already known. Third, the encounter with the holy in the person of Yahweh cannot be subsumed under universal religious experience, but must involve a recognition of his exclusive claim to holiness.

What we need is a theoretical framework for explaining the paradox of divine and human authorship of the rendering of God in Scripture. This is what the orthodox doctrine of inspiration was meant to accomplish, so our formulation of such a framework must assess the strengths and weaknesses of this doctrine and its liberal and neo-orthodox substitutes on the way to a new solution. This new solution should arise organically from the concepts that have been developed in this study of biblical God-language.

The formation of the canon of Scripture completes a significant phase in the rendering of God and inaugurates a new one. It is important to recognize the new mode of encountering the biblical God. By entering a book, Yahweh was no longer restricted to a single national tradition, but could enter the traditions of the Gentiles. The invitation to the peoples of the world to recognize the biblical God was extended under the authority of Jesus Christ. The New Testament claims that the God of Israel was present and active in the life, death and resurrection of Jesus to extend his reign to the ends of the earth.

SPEAKING OF INSPIRATION

The classical Christian doctrine of inspiration was devised to explain how the human authors of Scripture could communicate the word of God and to guarantee that such a communication did in fact take place. In opposition to this doctrine, liberal Christians have tended to view the biblical authors as gaining their insights in the same way the authors of nonbiblical literature do. The neo-orthodox theologians sought to transcend this antithesis by preserving divine initiative in self-revelation and human initiative in the interpretation of the events in which he was manifested. All of these attempted solutions embody legitimate concerns and have facilitated genuine encounter with the biblical God, but each fails to appreciate components of the biblical rendering of God.

The classical doctrine of inspiration was able to guarantee that Scripture was encountered as God's word by conceiving the human authors as passive instruments of God's communication. Whether the model employed to visualize the process was one of divine dictation or a more dynamic personal process of inner illumination, the creative role of the human mind and the relativities of human history were not appreciated. The doctrine of inspiration encouraged the appropriation of the Bible as a supernatural fact without the fallibility of humans, devoid of human ambiguity and uncertainty, and lacking in the dramatic interaction in which God achieves his identity.

The liberal theological movement accentuated precisely those aspects of biblical authorship which the orthodox doctrine ignored or denied. For the typical liberal, God is present everywhere and humans grow into awareness of him. The biblical story, thus, is one of human discovery of spiritual truths. Although the liberals found the earlier portions of Scripture too anthropomorphic and nationalistic for their tastes, they believed that they could observe a progressive spiritualization of Israelite monotheism which reaches a culmination in the New Testament conception of a loving God.

The liberal view is to be commended for introducing human activity and the movement of history into the process of authorship, but it has several severe defects. The biblical rendering of God is reduced to a concept, which misses entirely the existential encounter involved in biblical communication. Moreover, the liberal view makes the biblical God a human approximation of the divine, robbing him of his authority and urgency. If the rendering of God is to encounter us as a demanding and promising presence that requires of us a decision about our ultimate destiny, it must offer us the identity of God himself. Finally, the dynamic of recognition requires that the God of the present and future be known in tradition. Evolution or development is a misleading concept to apply to the process.

The neo-orthodox theologians—whose influence is evident on every page of this book—sought to preserve the insights of both orthodoxy and liberalism while transcending their defects. Chief emphasis was placed on the *self*-revelation of God.[1] Revelation, it was said, is not the communication of timeless truth nor the progressive discovery of spiritual concepts, but a divine-human encounter. In some neo-orthodox authors, it seems that the divine presence is without content, i.e., ineffable, so that the identity of God is a product of human reflection on the events in which his presence was manifested.[2] However, at least Karl Barth held that self-revelation included the identity of God.[3]

The neo-othodox theologoumenon of *self*-revelation is faulty in its

---

1. For this basic thesis, see John Baillie, *The Idea of Revelation in Recent Thought* (New York and London: Columbia University Press, 1956).

2. Buber and Bultmann tend in this direction. On Buber, compare the following note.

3. Note J. Moltmann's exposition in *Theology of Hope* (New York and Evanston: Harper & Row, 1967), pp. 54–57, particularly: "Self-revelation does not mean for Barth personalistic self-disclosure of God after the analogy of the I-Thou relationship between men. God reveals himself in actual fact as 'somebody' and 'something' for man, not as pure, absolute Thou. That would in any case, like the individual, be 'ineffable' " (p. 56).

attempt to preserve a dimension of direct revelation unmediated by the process of establishing and maintaining the identity of God. According to my analysis of characterization, presence can be established only in conjunction with the delineation of identity. Encounter with God is possible only through the interpretive tradition that renders his identity. History is the locus of revelation only where that history includes the tradition in which God is already known, but then it is not a matter of revelation of what would be otherwise unknown, but a finding of the one who is.[4]

If the arguments of this study of biblical God-language have been successful, we must begin with the proposition that the transcendent God has deigned to enter human consciousness as the dramatis persona of biblical literature. This is, I believe, the corollary of the argument that Yahweh is God indeed. If this is so, it follows that the act of human imagination which rendered him as a dramatis persona is the vehicle of God's act of establishing his identity among his creatures. To use John Calvin's expression, God has "accommodated" himself to human understanding by identifying with his dramatis persona.[5]

Now the question is: How is it possible for the human imagination to serve this purpose? I shall argue that the human imagination is in principle capable of such service, that the persona of the religious tradition maintained his identity in each act of rendering him, and that the course of history entered into his identity. In these ways God initiated the rendering of his identity by human authors. As a corollary, we can also affirm that the formation of biblical tradition was under his providential guidance.

The power of the imagination to render character vividly, maintain consistency of identity, grasp events as actions, and so forth,

4. J. Barr, *Old and New in Interpretation* (New York: Harper & Row, 1966), p. 82.
5. E.g., "(God) accommodates himself to our capacity in addressing us" and "for since he is in himself incomprehensible, he assumes, when he wishes to manifest himself to men, those marks by which he may be known." Cited by E. Dowey, *The Knowledge of God in Calvin's Theology* (New York: Columbia University Press, 1952), p. 4, n. 1. I am in essential agreement with Calvin on this subject, but I would want to insist the incomprehensibility of God is part of his identity. The one whom we encounter in the biblical rendering is the one whose "knowledge is too wonderful for me" (Ps. 139:6). For this reason, I would reject the process polarity of "primordial God" and "consequent God."

makes it a fit instrument of God's appearance as a dramatis persona in human history. Moreover, the imaginative rendering of character is not a willful act, but entails submitting to the demands imposed by characterization in the very act of creating character. This introduces responsibility into the creative act. When it is the task of rendering God, the responsibility is acute because he is the epitome of truth and right. Hence, the human imagination is capable of rendering responsible service to God's act of self-identification.

It would not have occurred to any biblical author or generation of Israelites that they were engaged in creating Yahweh in their writings and actions. Not only was this character such that as Creator and Lord he must be the sole author of his own identity, but also he was encountered as already possessing that identity in tradition. The identity established in tradition confronted each author and each generation as an objective reality. No one was free to imagine him as he pleased. Thus, the dramatis persona Yahweh stood over against those who were called to maintain his identity. We might say that the uncanny capacity of this "imaginary" character to retain a consistent identity through the vicissitudes of Israel's history is the literary/cultural principle of his self-determination.

Not only was the act of imagining Yahweh performed under the demands of characterization and the force of tradition, but it was also under the pressure of history. The events of the time were not simply occasions for recognizing the one who is always the same, but interactions between God and humans that entered into the very identity of the one already known. The God who was already known had to prove himself in the matters at hand. The authors of Scripture had to seek him in the course of human events to know who he is.

This historical pressure on the act of rendering God makes it possible to affirm the guidance of divine providence in the formation of tradition.[6] If God's action is found in the course of human events, human actions and natural coincidences must serve his purposes. The process of establishing and maintaining his identity would itself

---

6. J. Barr, *Old and New in Interpretation*, p. 156, offers this marvelous formulation: "The growth and development of tradition is soteriologically functional."

constitute a significant form of God's providential action. He, as it were, watches over the identity that is taking shape in Israelite tradition.

Not only the tradition, but also its human creators and bearers are under the guidance of providence. Yahweh is said to *call* individuals and nations to serve his purposes. When it is a foreign nation or ruler, there is no consciousness of being Yahweh's agent. When it is an Israelite, there is. Yahweh calls members of his people to speak in his behalf, to lead his people, to maintain his cultus, to enforce his law, and so forth. Involved in a call was the promise of God to watch over his word, provide wisdom and courage to the agent, and to bring his purposes to a successful conclusion. The formation of the tradition in which he is known is the cumulative result of his calls and the history generated by them.

The people of Israel as a whole was called to be Yahweh's treasured possession and servant nation. The election of Israel is the counterpart of the calls of individuals, for Yahweh was a common possession, the one "enthroned on the praises of Israel" (Ps. 22:3). This delightful image can serve as a metaphor for the existence of Yahweh in the collective imagination. The people served the divine purpose simply by recognizing him in their tradition, finding him in the course of their history, and recognizing him to be the source and ground of their religious and moral experience.

By way of summary, it can be confessed that God has established his identity and offered his presence in the biblical rendering of Yahweh. The arts of characterization and historical interpretation have been made vehicles of God's self-identification. The process took place under the guidance of a providence that called this people to recognize him.

THE PROCESS AND EFFECT OF CANONIZATION

The decision of the Jewish religious community to recognize the writings that compose Hebrew Scripture as uniquely authoritative and set apart from all other writings had the effect of stopping the process of rendering God that had produced the literature. In place of it there grew up a tradition that interpreted and adapted the biblical text to the ongoing questions of communal life. "The existence of a scripture has the effect of changing the character of tradition; the tradition continues indeed to develop but now assumes to a larger degree the character of an interpretation of the scripture."[7]

The principle of a canon or standard operative in theological tradition did not originate with canonization, but in fact existed from the very beginnings of Yahwism. Each new writing had to meet the standards of legitimacy built into the tradition in order to be accepted into it. When a writing was accepted, it became a part of the standard-setting tradition. The single most important standard was undoubtedly the identity of the rendering of Yahweh in it with the God already known. Those writings that were judged to meet this standard constituted the Scripture in formation.

There was no formal decision to set certain writings apart as Holy Scripture. Rather, the writings that had established themselves as preeminent within the legitimate tradition were gradually elevated into the status of inviolable texts and collected together as a single book. This book grew over centuries into the present lineaments of Hebrew Scripture and underwent something of a ratification at Jamnia and gained unassailable ascendency in Judaism with the victory of its Rabbinic partisans.

Although the Jewish community perceives something of a hierarchy within the Hebrew Bible, the book is meant to communicate as a single work. All God-language refers to the same persona and works in tandem to identify him. Furthermore, the material constitutes a single story united by the action of this God.

Scripture is also considered to be complete. This judgment is expressed in the idea that revelation ceased with Ezra.[8] The rendering of God in this body of literature is sufficient for the ongoing life of the community during the interim between the exile and the denouement of human history. Although the God of Israel continues to rule his creatures and determine individual and collective destiny, the events of history no longer enter into his identity. The identity of God has been established once and for all, open only to the com-

---

7. J. Barr, *The Bible in the Modern World* (New York: Harper & Row, 1973), p. 117.

8. Cf. O. Eissfeldt, *The Old Testament: An Introduction* (New York and Evanston: Harper & Row, 1965), pp. 563f., 568.

ing divine intervention to fulfill the prophetic hope of unconditional salvation.

Of course, God's entry into a book did not mean the end of the communal enterprise of encountering him as a dramatis persona in the tradition and recognizing this persona in the life of the present. The biblical God is not the sort of character who is exhausted in the literature rendering him. Rather, he calls a community into being to recognize him collectively in worship, study and daily living. Sociologically, a belief system requires a community that shares it and makes it plausible to individual members.[9] The God rendered in Scripture is the center of such a belief system, so he requires a community that shares in recognizing him and in reinforcing the conviction of his reality. Theologically, God elects a community in which to dwell.[10]

The biblical God could not sustain the conviction of a community if he were not recognized in the present as the one already known in Scripture. Since his identity was complete and the present was an interim between promise and fulfillment, the moment of recognition could not take the same form as it had in the course of biblical history. Now it took the form of a reenactment of the once for all scriptural events in such a way that they conformed to the contemporary sense of truth and the form of expansions of textual meaning to solve the problems of living among the Gentiles in the stream of world history. The Scripture, thus, generated a cultic and teaching tradition that purported to be an interpretation of its contents.[11]

God's entry into a book had the effect of freeing him for many peoples and diverse traditions. When the biblical tradition was in formation, he was bound to the community that cultivated the tradition. When the tradition became fixed in the canon of Scripture, he

9. Peter Berger, *The Sacred Canopy* (Garden City, N.Y.: Anchor/Doubleday & Co., 1967), pp. 45–48, 78–79, and elsewhere.

10. Compare the Jewish theologoumenon of the Shechinah, which is, however, faulty in separating the absolute and the divine identity that is immanent in the world, particularly in the holy community.

11. The employment of noncommentary formats—like Philo's and Josephus's writings—did not mean a fundamental departure from the "commentary" idea. Those who took their stand within the religious community sought to remain faithful to Scriptural teaching and oral tradition. The more acculturated thinkers simply sought to explain the tradition by means of current and original concepts, but not to alter or misrepresent it.

was free to move beyond a specific, socially defined entity. The Jewish religious community itself was so widely dispersed after the exile
that it could not have sustained the identity of the biblical God in its
traditions without a common, authoritative Scripture.[12] But the
existence of Scripture had a more radical potential as well, for it
facilitated the recognition by Gentiles of the biblical God apart from
the interpretive traditions and social structures of Judaism.

The existence of a Scripture was the precondition of the recognition of the biblical God by Christians and Muslims as well as Jews.
Through this book he has been made available to many peoples with
diverse traditions. The title, "Israel, the people of God," has been
expanded to include not only the national descendants of Israel but
also those among the nations who have been called into fellowship
with the biblical God.

When Gentiles join Jews in the recognition of the biblical God,
they take on the burden of establishing and maintaining his identity
in their cultic and teaching traditions. Hebrew Scripture becomes
their Scripture, and the rendering of God in it becomes the source
and norm of their God-language.

GOD'S INVITATION TO GENTILES

The existence of Scripture is the precondition of the God of
Israel becoming the God of the nations, but it is not the cause. The
full weight of Christian claims to Jesus' messiahship must be brought
to bear on Hebrew Scripture to accomplish it. To open Israel to
include the nations, Israel's God must act with eschatological finality
in the person of Jesus. In these concluding paragraphs I will medi-
tate on the logic of Christ's invitation to Gentiles to join the Jews in
recognizing God.

James Barr is quite right in asserting that the "Christian use of
the Old Testament seems to depend on the belief that the One God
who is the God of Israel is also the God and Father of Jesus Christ."[13]
This belief is indispensable for Christians, for Jesus himself called
the God of Scripture and Jewish tradition "Father" and discovered

---

12. This assertion is substantiated by the reversion to polytheism in the early
diaspora communities such as Elephantine.

13. *Old and New in Interpretation,* p. 149.

who he was in the reading of Scripture within a Jewish religious context.[14] In addition, the community that formed around him found the action of the biblical God in what Jesus did and suffered, and interpreted him in terms of the messianic expectations inaugurated in biblical prophecy and developed in Jewish tradition. If the God of the New Testament were not identical with the God of Hebrew Scripture, the Christian faith would topple for lack of a foundation.

The authors of the synoptic Gospels endeavor to evoke the scriptural context in which their story unfolds. They employ a variety of means, many of which have roots in ancient biblical and contemporary Jewish exegesis.[15] Background similarities are evoked, texts are quoted to express piety and dispute issues, prophecies are cited as being fulfilled, and acts are identified as fulfilling Scripture without citation. These devices can be viewed as aesthetic means for establishing the fundamental claim that the God of Scripture is present and active in the life of Jesus.[16] They achieve the desired effect through their cumulative metaphorical and mimetic power.

There is one radical difference between the depiction of God in Hebrew Scripture and the representation of reality in the New Testament. Jesus is the dramatic center of the Gospel narratives and epistolary proclamation, while God—the Father—is hidden. It is Jesus' identity that is established and maintained in this literature. It is the person of Jesus whose presence is evoked dramatically. God is present behind the scenes, seldom rendered as actor. This change of dramatic center, I believe, embodies the claim that God has identified with Jesus, that his presence is in this human, and that his action identifies this human. That is to say, the God of Israel is present and active in bestowing his authority on and identifying his cause with this humble man from Nazareth.[17]

The authors of the New Testament exhibit a strong drive to place

14. Ibid., pp. 157f.
15. Ibid., pp. 113–29.
16. It may be that the authors meant some citations and references as proof that Jesus is the one predicted, but this may be much less important than has been attributed to them by both Protestant orthodoxy and the liberal detractors. The debate over typology in the days of the biblical theology movement was probably a waste, for as an aesthetic principle it is hardly controversial.
17. Numerous paradoxical statements in the Gospel of John explain the replacement of God with Jesus, e.g., John 5:37–40; 14:9–10.

God's action in the life and person of Jesus within the sequential, cumulative story told in Hebrew Scripture. The story of God's action is rehearsed in Stephen's testimony before the Jewish authorities (Acts 7) and Paul grapples constantly with the dialectic of God's acts for Israel and in the Christ event (e.g., Romans 3, 4, 9—11; cf. 5, 7; Galatians 3; 4:21ff.). The placement of the story of Jesus within the comprehensive biblical drama further substantiates the claim that the biblical God has acted within it.

The claim that the biblical God was present and active in the life, death and resurrection of Jesus required that it be the culmination of all God's work. The story of God's action in history ends in the exile. There was no place for his continuing action in history because the prophets had announced Israel's judgment and a transformation of Israel and the nations that surpassed the conditions of history. The apocalyptic writers heightened the radicality of the transformation even further, generating the expectation of a new heaven and earth, the resurrection of the dead, a final judgment, and the establishment of God's eternal kingdom. Ongoing history could be nothing more than an interim between the judgment of Israel—the exile— and the resolution of the entire human drama. If Jesus' life, death and resurrection were to qualify as God's action, they must constitute the eschatological denouement. Nothing less could enter into the identity of the biblical God.

The same ultimacy is involved in the claim that Jesus is the Messiah. The royal traditions of the house of David had undergone a progressive transformation from ideology to eschatological promise. Only an eschatological figure could really bear the weight of the promises and powers vouchsafed the members of this dynasty. Isaiah evidently was the first person to realize this, and he inaugurated a messianic tradition that gathered momentum through later prophets and their apocalyptic successors. With the end of the Judaean monarchy, the royal traditions were perforce interpreted futuristically and it was a simple step to make his appearance the turning of the ages and his reign an eternal one. Finally, the figure generated variants—particularly among Jewish sects—which could feed back into mainstream expectations. The Jesus of the Gospels lays claim to messianic expectations and molds them to fit his intentionality.[18] The person of Jesus cannot be separated from the messianic claims which he made, which prompted his execution, which were confirmed by the resurrection, and which were proclaimed by the church.

The eschatological significance attached to Jesus both redeems the prophetic message of salvation and generates a crisis of confirmation for Christians. Since the truth of prophecy must be confirmed by fulfillment, the promises of salvation that run through all the classical prophets from Hosea on are under the threat of nullification. If Jesus is the Messiah of God, these promises have been confirmed. However, they must remain as promises, confirmed by the first coming but awaiting the second coming for fulfillment in power. The delay of Christ's return itself generates a crisis of confirmation for only when "he has put all his enemies under his feet" (1 Cor. 15:25) will he meet the qualifications of the Messiah of Jewish expectation.

Jews and Christians actually must live with very similar paradoxes. For the Jews, history is an interim between the unconfirmed prophetic promises and God's intervention, while for Christians it is an interim between the first and the second coming.[19] A Christian should, therefore, be quite sympathetic to the Jewish rejection of Jesus' messianic claims, for it corresponds to the crisis of confirmation with which Christians must live. Faith in Christ is indeed a gift of "conviction of things not seen" (Heb. 11:1).

Christians are not only called to hope, however; they are also called to enter the kingdom of God that exists in a hidden form in history. One aspect of the hidden kingdom is directly relevant to our subject: the invitation issued Gentiles to recognize the biblical God. Judaism could not do this. Non-Jews could become Jews and thereby enter into fellowship with God, but Gentiles qua Gentiles were outside the people called to recognize the living God in Scripture and

18. Hans Frei, in *The Identity of Jesus Christ* (Philadelphia: Fortress Press, 1967/1975), pp. 86ff., makes important observations about the way Jesus gradually and progressively assumes the office and defines it.
19. More sophisticated Jews and Christians are able to escape this paradox by either displacing eschatological hopes to another ontological realm or identifying these hopes with human progress and perfectibility, but they do so at some cost.

tradition. They would encounter this God only in the denouement of history. It was precisely because that denouement had occurred in the life, death and resurrection of Jesus that Christians could invite Gentiles to recognize the biblical God without becoming Jews and accepting the yoke of the Torah, i.e., Hebrew Scripture as interpreted by Jewish tradition. The community united by faith in Christ, constituting the vanguard of the kingdom, should transcend the distinction between Jew and Gentile—indeed, all ethnic, social, sexual, racial and political divisions among humans (Gal. 3:28).

The fact that Gentiles have come to the biblical God by way of Christ has often been taken to imply christological exegesis of the Old Testament. What this has often meant is a curtailment of the distinctive witness of the Old Testament. A more dialectical approach would be to read the Old Testament as complete and unified in itself but generative of the hope of the Messiah and hence applicable in the interpretation of Jesus.[20] The identity and reality of the biblical God is established in the rendering of this dramatis persona in the Scripture held in common by Jews, Christians and Muslims, and each community must maintain his identity in its tradition to establish its own legitimacy. On this basis, it was right and proper to limit this study of biblical God-language to the Scripture which Christians call the Old Testament.

20. This is approximately the position J. Barr develops in "Old and New Testaments in the Work of Salvation," *Old and New in Interpretation*, pp. 149ff.

Scripture Index